# knit on down™

HOUSE of
WHITE
BIRCHES

PUBLISHERS
SINCE 1947

# knit on down™

editor Jeanne Stauffer
art director Brad Snow
publishing services manager Brenda Gallmeyer

senior editor Kathy Wesley
managing editor Dianne Schmidt
assistant art director Nick Pierce
copy supervisor Michelle Beck
copy editors Mary O'Donnell, Susanna Tobias
technical editor Charlotte Quiggle
technical artist Nicole Gage

graphic arts supervisor Ronda Bechinski
graphic artists Jessi Butler, Minette Collins Smith
production assistants Marj Morgan,
Judy Neuenschwander

photography supervisor Tammy Christian
photography Matthew Owen
photography assistant Tammy Nussbaum

first printing: 2008, China
Library of Congress number: 2007936743
hardcover ISBN: 978-1-59217-210-8
softcover ISBN: 978-1-59217-211-5

Every effort has been made to ensure the accuracy and
completeness of the instructions in this book. However, we
cannot be responsible for human error or for the results
when using materials other than those specified in the
instructions, or for variations in individual work.

1 2 3 4 5 6 7 8 9

DRGbooks.com

Welcome to *Knit On Down!*

If you have already tried knitting from the top down, you have experienced the advantages of working a piece from the top down. If you haven't tried top-down knitting, you are in for a treat!

Have you ever knit a sweater that ended up the wrong length? With top-down knit sweaters, you can try it on as you go. So after the first part is knit, you can check the top. There is also the length-adjustment advantage. Sleeve and body length can be added to or ripped back without having to re-knit the whole sweater. For children, you can stop at the ideal length or even add some length when they grow. For socks, we think of the toe as the top (picture your feet up on an ottoman). You can try the sock on and decide when to start the heel shaping.

We've included a chapter of Knit on Down Tips to show you techniques that will help you make seaming a thing of the past—techniques like provisional cast-ons, adding stitches once knitting and working in rounds.

We've also included close-up photos of many of the stitch patterns. Keep in mind that in these close-up photos all stitches are displayed *as they are worn, i.e. the top of garment = the top of the stitch.*

To help you locate the perfect design need of the moment, we've organized our projects into these chapters: Sweaters for Every Season, Sweaters for Friends, Family & Pets, Togs for Baby & Toddler, Hats & Socks, and For Charity.

welcome

# contents

# knit on down tips

One of the reasons many knitters enjoy knitting from the top down is the lack of seams. Since the garment is worked in one piece, rather than in individual pieces (back, front, sleeves), the need for seams is almost entirely eliminated. With little need for finishing beyond blocking and weaving in ends, the garment is nearly complete when the last stitch is bound off. That said, there are some specific techniques that are very useful when working a garment from the top down.

## Important Tools

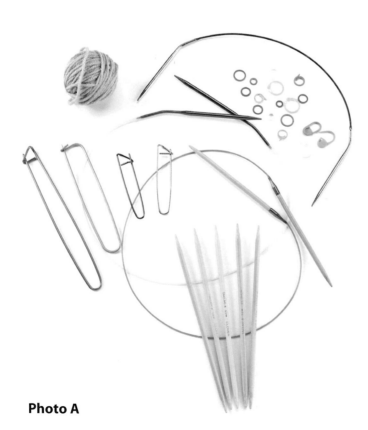

**Photo A**

**Stitch Markers** can be purchased in a store in many varieties, or the knitter can make her own by making little circles of different-colored yarns to slip on her needles. Markers have several uses, with one or more being used at the same time. When working in the round, one marker is used to indicate the beginning of the round. Other markers may also be used to separate a pattern stitch from other stitches, making it easier to identify the beginning and ending stitches of the pattern. Many of the patterns in this book use markers in the yoke area to indicate where increases are made for the front, back and sleeves. It is helpful to have a marker in a different or contrasting color (CC) to use at the beginning of the round.

To place a marker (pm) on the needle, just slip the marker (sm) onto the needle as indicated in the instructions. On the next row or round, work in the indicated pattern to the marker, then slip the marker by sliding it from one needle to the other and continue working the remaining stitches.

**Stitch holders** are used to hold some of the stitches while working other parts of the garment. Holders of many lengths are available for purchase. When a larger number of stitches is set aside, lengths of a smooth contrasting yarn of the same weight or slightly finer weight, referred to as *waste yarn*, can be used to hold the stitches.

**Circular needles** come in a variety of lengths. Usually more than one length is called for in a pattern. In some patterns, although part of the garment may be worked back and forth in rows, a circular needle is used to accommodate the large number of stitches; in this case, do not join the knitting to work in the round, instead work in the same manner as with straight needles, turning the work at the end of each row.

When working in the round, however, it is important to have a circular needle that will comfortably hold all the stitches, allowing for continuous knitting in the round. As the number of stitches increases or decreases, a longer or shorter needle is needed to avoid the bunching or stretching of the stitches.

**Double-pointed needles** (dpns) are used when working in the round and when there are too few stitches to fit comfortably on a circular needle.

### Special Techniques
### Provisional Cast On (Method 1)

A number of garments in this book start with a provisional cast on. This technique is used because the cast-on edge will eventually be removed, revealing "live" stitches which are then worked in the opposite direction. There are several methods for working a provisional cast on. The one shown in photo B is used throughout the book. You may wish to try one of the other provisional cast on methods for any of these projects.

This first method of working a provisional cast on starts with a crochet chain using a crochet hook about the same size as the knitting needle needed for the project. The table given below lists the crochet hook sizes that correspond most closely to knitting needle sizes.

| Crochet Hook | Knitting Needle |
| --- | --- |
| E/4 (3.5mm) | 4 (3.5mm) |
| F/5 (3.75mm) | 5 (3.75mm) |
| G/6 (4mm) | 6 (4mm) |
| H/8 (5mm) | 8 (5mm) |
| I/9 (5.5mm) | 9 (5.5mm) |
| J/10 (6mm) | 10 (6mm) |
| K/10½ (6.5mm) | 10½ (6.5mm) |

To work this type of provisional cast on, start with a smooth waste yarn and crochet a chain several stitches longer than the number of stitches to be cast on for the pattern you are working.

Once the chain is completed, cut the waste yarn, leaving a 4-inch tail, and pull the tail through the last loop. Put a knot in this tail to mark the end that you will unravel later.

Use a knitting needle to pick up and knit in the back bump of each chain (Photo B). Try not to split the yarn of the crochet chain because that will make it more difficult to "unzip" later.

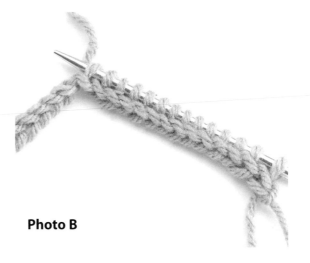

**Photo B**

Once the required number of stitches is on the needle, continue following the given instructions.

Later in the instructions, the provisional cast on chain is "unzipped" and live stitches are placed on the needle so the piece can be worked in the opposite direction.

To unzip the provisional cast on, hold the piece with the cast-on edge at the top. Begin with the last stitch cast on and gently pull out the chain, inserting the knitting needle into each stitch below the chain (Photo C).

**Photo C**

Continuing "unzipping" the chain until all the stitches are on the needle and follow the instructions for working in the opposite direction.

## Provisional Cast On (Method 2)
This method also uses a crochet hook and waste yarn but does not start with a chain stitch. The chart given for Method 1 on page 7 can be used in selecting the correct size crochet hook to use for this method as well. With smooth waste yarn, make a slip knot on the crochet hook (this loop is not counted as a stitch). Hold the knitting needle in the left hand, the crochet hook in the right hand and the yarn behind the needle. Place the crochet hook in front of the needle, hook the yarn and draw over the needle through the loop on the hook, making a stitch on the knitting needle.

Take the yarn back behind the needle and repeat this process until you have the desired number of stitches cast on (Photo D). Slip the last loop from the hook to the needle.

**Photo D**

Follow the instructions for completing the project. When working in the opposite direction "unzip" the provisional cast on carefully placing the "live" stitches onto the needle.

## Provisional Cast On (Method 3)
This method uses knitting needles instead of a crochet hook for the cast-on edge. After working the stitches in the opposite direction, the waste yarn does not unzip as for the other methods but needs to be snipped and pulled out.

Cast on with smooth waste yarn using a long-tail cast on. Knit a round, if working in rounds, or purl a row, if working in rows. Cut the waste yarn, change to color used for the garment and follow the given instructions (Photo E).

**Photo E**

When working in the opposite direction, hold the work with the cast on edge at the top and roll the edge so you can see the loops of the first round/row of stitches. Knit one stitch in each loop of the garment color (Photo F), taking care not to split the yarn.

**Photo F**

Once the remainder of the garment is complete, carefully snip through the stitch of the knitted round about every 10 stitches and gently pull out the waste yarn.

*Tip: You may find that shoulders that are worked down from provisional cast-ons are prone to stretching because there is no seam. To help prevent such stretching, tack grosgrain ribbon or a 3-stitch I-cord to the wrong side of the garment across the shoulders.*

### Adding Cast On Stitches

When a garment is started from the top, it is sometimes necessary to add stitches for the underarm on the armhole or sleeve edge. Since the yarn is already attached, a different method of casting on is used in this area. Again, there is more than one method for adding these stitches.

### Backward Loop Cast On

This method adds stitches at the end of the right-hand needle or the end of the row.

Bring the yarn around your left thumb

creating a loop. Slide the loop onto the needle (Photo G), pulling slightly on the yarn tail to tighten the loop.

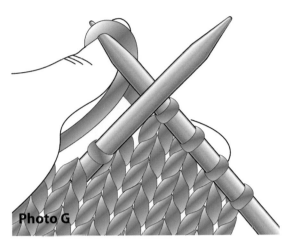

**Photo G**

### Knitted Cast On

This method adds stitches at the beginning of the left-hand needle or the beginning of the row.

Insert the right-hand needle from front to back into the first stitch on the left-hand needle. Wrap the yarn around the right-hand needle as if to knit and draw the yarn through the loop, but do not drop the loop from the left-hand needle (Photo H).

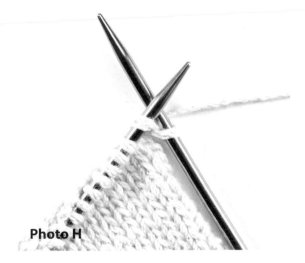

**Photo H**

Slip the loop just made onto the left-hand needle (Photo I).

**Photo I**

Continue in this manner for the desired number of stitches.

### Cable Cast On

The cable cast-on method also adds stitches at the beginning of the left-hand needle or the beginning of the row. The cable cast-on edge is more elastic and works well for ribbed edges. This method can also be used in place of the long-tail cast on at the beginning of a piece by starting with a slip knot.

Insert the right-hand needle from front to back into the first stitch on the left-hand needle. Wrap the yarn around the right-hand needle as if to knit and draw the yarn through the loop, but do not drop the loop from the left-hand needle. Slip the loop just made onto the left-hand needle.

Insert the right-hand needle between these two stitches and under the left-hand needle (Photo J).

Wrap the yarn around the right-hand needle as if to knit and pull the loop through, placing the loop on the left-hand needle (Photo K). Continue by placing the right-hand needle between the last two stitches on the left-hand needle for the desired number of stitches.

**Photo K**

### Working in Rounds vs. Rows

When working in rounds on either circular or double-pointed needles, it is important to remember that the right side is always facing you. The joined piece is creating a tube; you don't turn the work at the end of each row from right side to wrong side. This means that when working stockinette stitch in the round, you will knit every round instead of knitting the right-side rows and purling the wrong-side rows as when working back and forth on straight needles. Many like working in rounds for this very reason.

**Photo J**

However, to create the garter stitch when working in the round, alternate a round of knitting with a round of purling, rather than knitting every row as you would when working back and forth on straight needles. When joining the cast-on stitches, be sure that the "bottom" of all cast-on stitches are lying on the inside of the needle and not spiraled around it (Photo L).

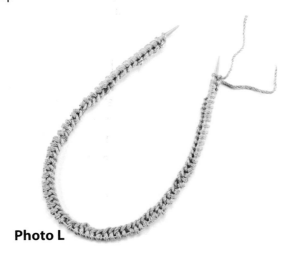

**Photo L**

Once joined, if the circle of stitches is twisted, there is no way to make your fabric back into a "tube" without ripping it back to the beginning and starting over. For this reason, it's a good idea to double-check that your knitting isn't twisted after you've worked a few rounds.

**Photo M**

A stitch marker is placed on the needle to identify the beginning of the round. Each

time the marker is reached, a round is completed. Slip the marker from one needle to the other and continue beginning a new round (Photo M).

Once the round is joined, additional markers may be placed on the needle to indicate the position of a pattern stitch or the spot where shaping will occur. It is helpful to make these markers a different color from the "beginning of round" marker (Photo N). Working from the top down (either in the round or back and forth in rows), when you get to the bottom of the body or sleeve (whichever is worked last), the piece is nearly complete. For some of the garments it may be necessary to go back and work an underarm or sleeve seam, but for others the garment is done and ready for weaving in ends and blocking. Once it's blocked, you can put it on and show it off!

**Photo N**

# sweaters for every season

These updated classics

include winter weights,

transitional styles

and lacy patterns for

warmer weather.

# allover cabling

**Design by Joyce Nordstrom**

The timeless appeal of a classic cardigan hits just the right textural note with easy cabling without a cable needle.

## Skill Level
■■■□ INTERMEDIATE

## Sizes
Woman's small (medium, large, extra-large, 2X-large, 3X-large) Instructions are given for smallest size, with larger sizes in parentheses. When only 1 number is given, it applies to all sizes.

## Finished Measurements
**Chest:** 37¾ (39½, 43, 46¼, 50¼, 53¼) inches (buttoned)
**Length:** 25½ (26¼, 27¾, 28¼, 30½, 31½) inches

## Materials
▼ Moda Dea Bamboo Wool 55 percent rayon from bamboo/45 percent wool medium weight yarn (145 yds/80g per ball): 8 (9, 10, 11, 12, 13) balls chili pepper #3920
▼ Size 5 (3.75mm) 29-inch circular needle
▼ Size 7 (4.5mm) 29- and 36-inch circular needles or size needed to obtain gauge
▼ 8 stitch markers
▼ Tapestry needle
▼ 6 (¾-inch) buttons

## Gauge
20 sts and 25 rows = 4 inches/10cm in St st with larger needle
To save time, take time to check gauge.

## Special Abbreviations
**Pm:** Place marker.
**Sm:** Sl marker.
**C3F (Cable 3 Front):** Skip 2 sts and knit the next st, leaving on needle; knit the 2 skipped sts.
**Inc1 (lifted increase):** At beg of row and following marker: K1, k1 in st 2 rows below st on RH needle; at end of row and before marker: K1 in row below next st on LH needle, then knit st on LH needle.

## Pattern Stitch
**Ribbed Cable** (multiple of 6 sts)
**Rows 1 and 3 (RS):** *K3, p3; rep from * to end.
**Row 2 and all WS rows:** Work the sts as they present themselves, knitting the knit sts, purling the purl sts.
**Row 5:** C3F, p3.
**Row 6:** Rep Row 2.
Rep Rows 1–6 for pat.

## Pattern Notes

This raglan cardigan begins at neck and is worked down to underarm, at which point the pieces are separated into sleeves and body, which are then worked separately. The front band is incorporated into the sweater and not worked separately.

The single sts between markers are raglan seams and are worked in St st throughout.

When working incs into pat on fronts, the st pat should mirror sleeve sts on other side of raglan seam.

Pat is worked back and forth in rows; a circular needle is used to accommodate the large number of sts.

## Instructions
### Yoke
Loosely cast on 67 (67, 73, 73, 79, 79) sts. Do not join.

**Raglan set-up row (WS):** Purl row, placing markers as follows: 3 front sts, pm, 1 raglan seam st, pm, 11 (11, 13, 13, 15, 15) sleeve sts, pm, 1 raglan seam st, pm, 35 (35, 37, 37, 39, 39) back sts, pm, 1 raglan seam st, pm, 11 (11, 13, 13, 15, 15) sleeve sts, pm, 1 raglan seam st, pm, 3 front sts.

### Shape Neck
**Pat set-up row (RS):** Inc1, p1 (p1, k1, k1, k1, k1), Inc1, sm, k1, sm, Inc1, k0 (0, 1, 1, 2, 2), p3, k3, p3, k0 (0, 1, 1, 2, 2), Inc1, sm, k1, sm, Inc1, k0 (0, 1, 1, 2, 2), [p3, k3] 5 times, p3, k0 (0, 1, 1, 2, 2), Inc1, sm, k1, sm, Inc1, k0 (0, 1, 1, 2, 2), p3, k3, p3, k 0 (0, 1, 1, 2, 2), Inc1, sm, k1, sm, Inc1, p1 (p1, k1, k1, k1, k1), Inc1. (77, 77, 83, 83, 89, 89 sts)

**Row 3 (and all WS rows):** Work Ribbed Cable pat as established, working new sts into pat as they accumulate (see Pattern Notes).

**Row 4 (Inc row):** *Inc1, work in pat as established to 1 st before marker, Inc1, sm,

k1, sm; rep from * to last marker, Inc1, work in pat as established to last st, Inc1. (87, 87, 93, 93, 99, 99 sts)

Rep Inc row [every other row] 6 (6, 8, 8, 10, 10) more times, ending with a WS row. (147, 147, 173, 173, 199, 199 sts)

## Front Band
**Next row (RS):** Cast on 8 sts for front band, pm, *work in pat to 1 st before marker, Inc1, sm, k1, sm, Inc1; rep from *, then work in pat to end, pm, cast on 8 sts for front band. (171, 171, 197, 197, 223, 223 sts)

**Next row:** K8, work in pat as established to last 8 sts, k8.

When front band measures 3 inches, work buttonhole on right front band as follows: k3, yo, k2tog, k3; rep buttonhole [every 4 inches] 4 times.

*At the same time,* maintaining first and last 8 sts in garter st for band, continue to inc on either side of raglan seam st [every other row] 21 (23, 24, 26, 29, 31) more times, ending with a WS row. (339, 355, 389, 405, 455, 471 sts)

Cut yarn.

## Separate sections
Removing markers, sl left front sts + raglan

seam st, left sleeve sts, back + 2 raglan seam sts, and right front + raglan seam st to separate pieces of waste yarn for holders. Right sleeve sts rem on needle.

## Right Sleeve
**Row 1 (RS):** Cast on 0 (0, 0, 2, 1, 3) sts, work in pat across right sleeve sts, cast on 0 (0, 0, 2, 1, 3) sts. (71, 75, 83, 91, 101, 109 sts)

Work 5 rows even.

**Dec row (RS):** K1, k2tog, work in pat to last 3 sts, ssk, k1.

Rep Dec row [every 6th row] 9 (9, 7, 4, 2, 0) times, then [every 4th row] 6 (7, 11, 14, 20, 23) times. (39, 41, 45, 53, 55, 61 sts)

Work even until sleeve measures 15 (15¼, 15½, 15¾, 16, 16¼) inches or 2 inches less than desired length.

Change to smaller needle and work even for 2 inches, ending with a RS row.

Loosely bind off in pat. Sew sleeve seam.

## Left Sleeve
Sl sts for left sleeve to larger needle and work as for right sleeve.

## Body
Sl all sts for fronts and back to larger needle.

**Next row (RS):** Work in pat as established across front, pick up and knit 0 (0, 0, 4, 1, 5) sts from underarm, work in pat across back, pick up and knit 0 (0, 0, 4, 1, 5) sts for underarm, work in pat as established across front. (197, 205, 223, 239, 259, 275 sts)

Work in pat as established, continuing to work buttonholes where required, until piece measures 14 (14, 14½, 14½, 15, 15½) inches from underarm, or 2 inches less than desired length.

Change to smaller needle and work even for 2 inches.

Bind off very loosely in pat.

## Finishing
### Neckband
With RS facing and using smaller needle, pick up and knit 8 sts across front band; 14 (14, 17, 17, 20, 20) sts to first seam st; 11 (11, 13, 13, 15, 15) sts across sleeve; 35 (35, 37, 37, 39, 39) sts across back; 11 (11, 13, 13, 15, 15) sts across sleeve; 14 (14, 17, 17, 20, 20) sts to front band; and 8 sts across front band. (101, 101, 113, 113, 125, 125 sts)

Work in k1, p1 rib for 2 inches, placing buttonhole on right front 1 inch from beg of picked up sts.

Bind off loosely in pat. Sew buttons opposite buttonholes. Weave in all ends. Block to finished measurements. ▼

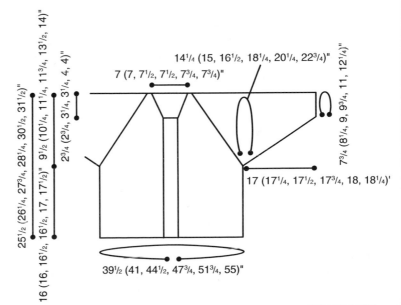

# saddle-shoulder tunic

**Design by Carol May**

## The interest starts at the shoulders and continues on down for an impressive silhouette.

**Skill Level**

◼◼◼◻ INTERMEDIATE

**Sizes**

Woman's small (medium, large, extra-large) Instructions are given for smallest size, with larger sizes in parentheses. When only 1 number is given, it applies to all sizes.

**Finished Measurements**

**Chest:** 38 (42½, 46¼, 48¼) inches
**Length:** 30 inches

**Materials**

- ▼ Plymouth/Cleckheaton Country 8 Ply Naturals 100 percent superwash wool light weight yarn (105 yds/50g per ball): 15 (17, 20, 21) balls blue tweed #1815
- ▼ Size 5 (3.75mm) double-pointed, 16- and 29-inch circular needles
- ▼ Size 6 (4mm) double-pointed, 16- and 29-inch circular needles or size needed to obtain gauge
- ▼ Cable needle
- ▼ Stitch markers
- ▼ Stitch holders
- ▼ Tapestry needle

**Gauge**

24 sts and 28 rows = 4 inches/10cm in charted rib and cable pat in pat using larger needles
To save time, take time to check gauge.

**Special Abbreviations**

**C4F (Cable 4 Front):** Sl 2 to cn and hold in front, k2, k2 from cn.
**C4B (Cable 4 Back):** Sl 2 to cn and hold in back, k2, k2 from cn.
**W6 (Wrap 6):** Sl 6 to cn and wrap yarn around the sts clockwise twice, then k6 from cn.
**M1 (Make 1):** Insert LH needle from front to back under horizontal strand between last st worked and next st, with RH needle, knit in back of lp.

**Pattern Stitches**

**A. Wrapped Rib St** (multiple of 8 sts + 10)
**Row 1 (RS):** P2, *k2, p2; rep from * across.
**Row 2 and all WS rows:** K2, *p2, k2; rep from * across.
**Row 3:** P2, *W6, p2; rep from * across.
**Row 5:** Rep Row 1.
**Row 7:** P2, k2, p2, *W6, p2; rep from * once, end k2, p2.
**Row 8:** Rep Row 2.
Rep Rows 1–8 for pat.

**B. Cable and Rib** (see Charts)

**Pattern Notes**
Sweater is worked in 1 piece, starting with the saddle shoulders. The back and front yokes are picked up from the shoulders and worked back and forth, then joined; lower body is worked in the round. The sleeves are worked in the rnd from the armhole.

The saddle-shoulder pieces should be oriented so that cast-on edges are at neck.

Remember that cables cross in opposite directions either side of center on back, front (after joining) and sleeves.

Change to longer circular needles or dpns when sts no longer fit comfortably on the needle in use.

**Instructions**
**Saddle Shoulders**
**Make 2**
With larger needles, cast on 26 sts.

Work 5 (6, 7, 7) reps of Wrapped Rib St, then cut yarn and place on holder.

**Back Yoke**
With RS facing, using larger circular needle and beg at edge with st holder, pick up and knit 33 (44, 50, 53) sts from long side of 1 shoulder piece; cast on 49 (39, 39, 39) sts for back neck; beg at cast-on edge, pick up and knit 33 (44, 50, 53) sts from side of other shoulder piece. (115, 127, 139, 145 sts)

Mark center st.

**Rows 1 (WS):** Beg and end where indicated on Chart A for size being worked, work pat across.

Continue in pat as established until piece measures 7½ (8, 8½, 8½) inches from shoulder piece, ending with a WS row.

Sl all sts to holder or waste yarn.

**Left Front Yoke**
With RS facing, using larger needle and beg at cast-on edge, pick up and knit 33 (44, 50, 53) sts along other side of shoulder piece.

**Row 1 (WS):** Beg and end where indicated on Chart B for size being worked, work across.

Work 2 rows even.

**Shape Neck**
**Inc row (RS):** K1, M1, work in pat as established to end. (34, 45, 51, 54 sts)

Rep Inc row [every 4th row] 4 (11, 11, 11) times, then [every other row] 16 (4, 4, 4) times, working new sts in pat as established and crossing new cables when there are enough sts to do so. (54, 60, 66, 69 sts)

Work even until piece measures 7½ (8, 8½, 8½) inches from shoulder piece, ending with same WS row as for back.

Cut yarn and sl sts to holder or waste yarn.

**Right Front Yoke**
With RS facing, using larger needle and beg at st holder, pick up and knit 33 (44, 50, 53) sts along other side of shoulder piece.

**Row 1 (WS):** Beg and end where indicated on Chart C for size being worked, work in pat across.

Work 2 rows even.

**Shape Neck**
**Inc row (RS):** Work in pat as established to last st, M1, k1. (34, 45, 51, 54 sts)

Rep Inc row [every 4th row] 4 (11, 11, 11) times, then [every other row] 16 (4, 4, 4) times, working new sts in pat as established and crossing new cables when there are enough sts to do so. (54, 60, 66, 69 sts)

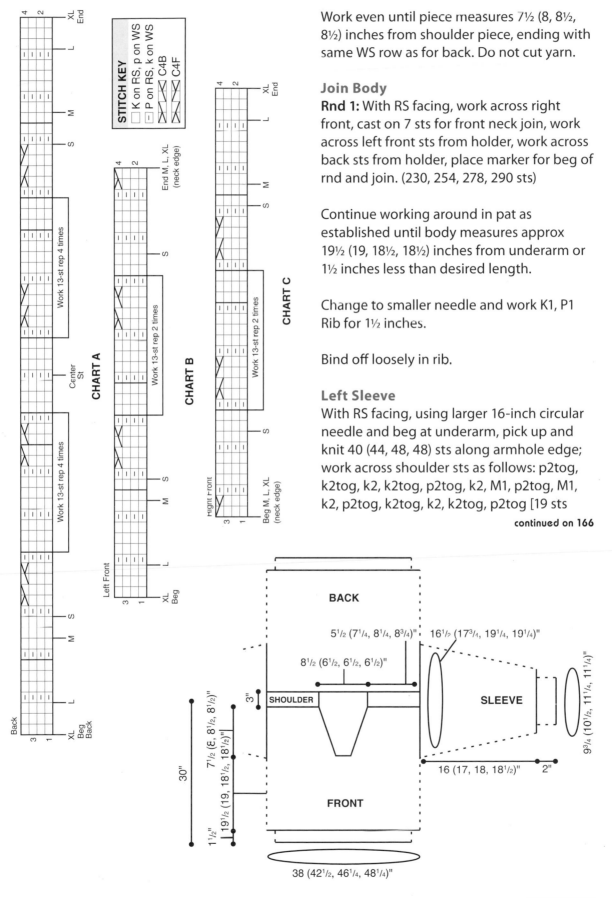

**STITCH KEY**

| | |
|---|---|
| ☐ K on RS, p on WS | ⬚ C4B |
| ⊟ P on RS, k on WS | ⬚ C4F |

**CHART A**

**CHART B**

**CHART C**

Work even until piece measures 7½ (8, 8½, 8½) inches from shoulder piece, ending with same WS row as for back. Do not cut yarn.

**Join Body**

**Rnd 1:** With RS facing, work across right front, cast on 7 sts for front neck join, work across left front sts from holder, work across back sts from holder, place marker for beg of rnd and join. (230, 254, 278, 290 sts)

Continue working around in pat as established until body measures approx 19½ (19, 18½, 18½) inches from underarm or 1½ inches less than desired length.

Change to smaller needle and work K1, P1 Rib for 1½ inches.

Bind off loosely in rib.

**Left Sleeve**

With RS facing, using larger 16-inch circular needle and beg at underarm, pick up and knit 40 (44, 48, 48) sts along armhole edge; work across shoulder sts as follows: p2tog, k2tog, k2, k2tog, p2tog, k2, M1, p2tog, M1, k2, p2tog, k2tog, k2, k2tog, p2tog [19 sts

continued on 166

BACK

5½ (7¼, 8¼, 8¾)"

8½ (6½, 6½, 6½)"

16½ (17¾, 19¼, 19¼)"

3"

SHOULDER

SLEEVE

FRONT

30"

7½ (8, 8½, 8½)"

1½"

19½ (19, 18½, 18½)"

9¾ (10½, 11¼, 11¼)"

16 (17, 18, 18½)"    2"

38 (42½, 46¼, 48¼)"

# winter sky cardigan

Design by Susan Robicheau

Take the chill off in a cool shade of blue, or choose a favorite shade to accent your wardrobe.

## Skill Level

■■■□ INTERMEDIATE

## Sizes

Woman's extra-small (small, medium, large, extra-large) Instructions are given for smallest size, with larger sizes in parentheses. When only 1 number is given, it applies to all sizes.

## Finished Measurements

**Chest:** 34¾ (35¾, 40¾, 44, 48) inches (buttoned)
**Length:** 22 (23, 24, 25, 26) inches

## Materials

- ▼ Bernat Cashmere 65 percent acrylic/30 percent nylon/5 percent cashmere) medium weight yarn (103 yds/60g per ball): 9 (11, 13, 14, 16) balls rain #16143
- ▼ Size 5 (3.75mm) 29-inch circular needle
- ▼ Size 7 (4.5mm) double-point, 16- and 29-inch (or longer) circular needles or size needed to obtain gauge
- ▼ Large crochet hook
- ▼ Waste yarn
- ▼ Stitch markers
- ▼ Tapestry needle
- ▼ 6 (½-inch) buttons

## Gauge

17 sts and 28 rows = 4 inches/10cm in Seed St with larger needle
To save time, take time to check gauge.

## Special Abbreviation

**Dec1 (Decrease 1):** K2tog or p2tog as necessary to maintain Seed St pat.

## Special Technique

**Provisional Cast On:** With crochet hook and waste yarn, make a chain several sts longer than desired cast on. With knitting needle and project yarn, pick up indicated number of sts in the "bumps" on back of chain. When indicated in pat, "unzip" the crochet chain to free live sts.

## Pattern Stitches

**A. Border** (worked back and forth in rows, multiple of 10 sts)
**Row 1 (RS):** P4, k1, p1, k4.
**Row 2:** P3, k2, p2, k3.
**Row 3:** P2, k2, p1, k1, p2, k2.
**Row 4:** P1, k2, p2, k2, p2, k1.
**Row 5:** K2, p3, k3, p2.
**Row 6:** K1, p4, k4, p1.
Rep Rows 1–6 for pat.
**B. Border** (worked in rnds, multiple of 10 sts)

**Rnd 1 (RS):** *P4, k1, p1, k4; rep from * around.
**Rnd 2:** *P3, k2, p2, k3; rep from * around.
**Rnd 3:** *P2, k2, p1, k1, p2, k2; rep from * around.
**Rnd 4:** *P1, k2, p2, k2, p2, k1; rep from * around.
**Rnd 5:** *K2, p3, k3, p2; rep from *around.
**Rnd 6:** *K1, p4, k4, p1; rep from * around.
Rep Rnds 1–6 for pat.
**C. Seed St**
**Row 1 (RS):** *P1, k1; rep from * across.
**Row 2:** Knit the purl sts and purl the knit sts as they face you.
Rep Row 2 for pat.

### Pattern Notes

This raglan cardigan is worked from the yoke down. After the sleeves are separated from the body, the body is worked down. The sleeves are worked in the rnd from the underarms.

Yoke and body are worked back and forth; a circular needle is used to accommodate the large number of sts.

For sleeves, change to dpns when sts no longer fit comfortably on circular needle.

A chart for the Border pat is provided for those preferring to work from charts; when working in the rnd, read each rnd from right to left.

If desired, isolate Border pat by placing markers that are a different color from raglan markers between Border pat and Seed St.

Edge sts are worked in garter st throughout.

Raglan seam sts are worked in St st.

### Yoke

Using provisional method and larger 29-inch circular needle, cast on 98 (110, 126, 136, 150) sts; do not join.

**Set-up row (RS):** K1 [edge st], work Border pat over next 10 sts, work Seed St over 5 (7, 10, 12, 13) sts [front], place marker, k1 [raglan seam], place marker, work Seed St over 16 (18, 20, 21, 26) sts [sleeve], place marker, k1 [raglan seam], place marker, work Seed St over 30 (34, 40, 44, 46) sts [back], place marker, k1 [raglan seam], place marker, work Seed St over 16 (18, 20, 21, 26) sts [sleeve], place marker, k1, [raglan seam], place marker, Seed St 5 (7, 10, 12, 13) [front], work Border pat over next 10 sts, k1 [edge st].

**Row 2:** Work across in pats as established, maintaining edge sts in garter st and raglan seam sts in St st.

**Raglan Inc row:** *Work pats as established to marker, M1, sl marker, k1, sl marker, M1; rep from * across, then work pats as established to end. (106, 118, 134, 144, 158 sts)

Continue pats as established and rep Raglan Inc row [every 4th row] 13 (11, 12, 13, 16) times, working new sts into Seed St as established. (210, 206, 230, 248, 286 sts)

Work fronts and back even without inc, but continue to inc in sleeve sections as before [every 4th row] 0 (2, 3, 2, 0) times. (210, 214, 242, 256, 286 sts)

Work even until yoke measures approx 8 (8½, 9, 9½, 10) inches, ending a WS row.

### Separate Body & Sleeves

**Next row (RS):** Removing raglan markers, work to 2nd marker, sl 44 (46, 52, 53, 60) sleeve sts to waste yarn, cast on 12 (14, 16, 17, 18) underarm sts, k1, work to next marker, k1, sl 44 (46, 52, 53, 60) sleeve sts to waste yarn, cast on 12 (14, 16, 17, 18) underarm sts, work to end of row. (146, 150, 170, 184, 202 sts)

### Body

Working underarm sts in Seed St as established, work even until body measures approx 9 (9½, 10, 10½, 11) inches, or 5 inches short of desired length, ending with Row 5 of Border pat.

**Next row:** K1, work Border pat as established, dec 4 (inc 2, inc 2, dec 2, --) sts evenly spaced in Seed St section, work Border pat, k1. (142, 152, 172, 182, 202 sts)

## Bottom Band

**Row 1 (RS):** K1 (edge st), work 14 (15, 17, 18, 20) reps of Border pat to last st, k1 (edge st).

Work even in Border pat until band measures approx 5 inches, ending with Row 6.

Bind off loosely.

## Sleeves

Sl 44 (46, 52, 53, 60) sleeve sts from waste yarn to larger 16-inch circular needle.

**Rnd 1:** Beg at center underarm, pick up and knit 6 (7, 8, 8, 9) sts from underarm, work across sleeve sts, pick up and knit 6 (7, 8, 9, 9) sts from underarm, place marker for beg of rnd and join. (56, 60, 68, 70, 78 sts)

Continuing in Seed St as established and working underarm sts into pat, work 6 (1, 6, 1, 6) rnd(s) even.

**Dec rnd:** Dec1, work in pat to last 2 sts, Dec1. (54, 58, 66, 68, 76 sts)

Continue in pat and rep Dec rnd [every 7th (6th, 6th, 6th, 7th) rnd] 12 (14, 13, 14, 13) times. (30, 30, 40, 40, 50 sts)

Work even until sleeve measures approx 14 (14, 14½, 14½, 15) inches or 3 inches less than desired length from underarm.

## Cuff

Work 3 (3, 4, 4, 5) reps of Border pat around until cuff measures approx 3 inches, ending with Rnd 6.

Bind off loosely.

## Neckband

Unzip crochet chain and sl 98 (110, 126, 136, 150) live sts to smaller 29-inch circular needle.

**Set-up row (RS):** K16 (18, 21, 23, 24), place marker, k16 (18, 20, 21, 26), place marker, k31 (35, 41, 45, 47), place marker, k16 (18, 20, 21, 26), place marker, k14 (16, 19, 21, 22).

**Dec row:** *Knit to 2 sts before marker, k2tog; rep from * to last marker, knit to end. (94, 106, 122, 132, 146 sts)

Working in garter st, rep Dec row [every other row] 4 times. (78, 90, 106, 116, 130 sts)

Bind off.

**continued on 166**

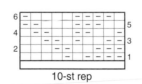

10-st rep

**STITCH KEY**
☐ K on RS, p on WS
⊟ P on RS, k on WS

**Winter Sky Cardigan**

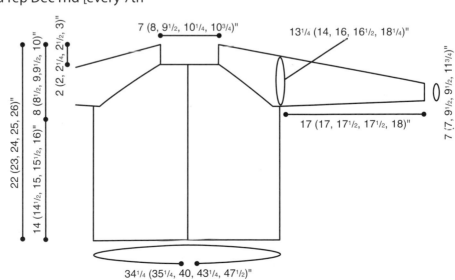

7 (8, 9½, 10¼, 10¾)"

13¼ (14, 16, 16½, 18¼)"

2 (2, 2¼, 2½, 3)"

8 (8½, 9, 9½, 10)"

22 (23, 24, 25, 26)"

14 (14½, 15, 15½, 16)"

7 (7, 9½, 9½, 11¾)"

17 (17, 17½, 17½, 18)"

34¼ (35¼, 40, 43¼, 47½)"

# joy-to-wear cardi

Design by Joyce Nordstrom

Feminine in its gentle ribbed shaping and mini-lace edgings, this cardigan will be a favorite.

## Skill Level
■■■□ INTERMEDIATE

## Sizes
Woman's small (medium, large, extra-large, 2X-large, 3X-large) Instructions are given for smallest size, with larger sizes in parentheses. When only 1 number is given, it applies to all sizes.

## Finished Measurements
**Chest:** 36½ (40½, 45½, 48½, 52½, 55¾) inches (buttoned)
**Length:** 25½ (25¾, 26½, 27¼, 28, 29) inches

## Materials
▼ TLC Cotton Plus 51 percent cotton/49 percent acrylic medium weight yarn (178 yds/100g per ball): 6 (6, 7, 8, 9, 10) balls medium rose #3707
▼ Size 5 (3.75mm) 29-inch (or longer) circular needle
▼ Size 7 (4.5mm) 29-inch (or longer) circular needle or size needed to obtain gauge
▼ Stitch holders
▼ Stitch markers
▼ Tapestry needle
▼ 5 (¾-inch) buttons

## Gauge
20 sts and 25 rows = 4 inches/10cm in St st with larger needles
To save time, take time to check gauge.

## Pattern Stitches
**A. K4, P2 Rib** (multiple of 6 sts + 4)
**Row 1 (RS):** *K4, p2; rep from * to last 4 sts, k4.
**Row 2:** *P4, k2; rep from * to last 4 sts, p4.
Rep Rows 1 and 2 for pat.
**B. Beaded Edging** (multiple of 6 sts + 4, dec to 5 sts + 3)
**Row 1 (RS):** *K2tog, yo, ssk, p2; rep from * to last 4 sts, k2tog, yo, ssk. (1 st dec in each 4-st rib)
**Row 2:** *P3, k2; rep from * to last 3 sts, p3.
**Rows 3 and 5:** Knit.
**Row 4:** Purl.

*Note: When working Beaded Edging, always work [k2tog, yo, ssk] in K4 section of rib.*

## Pattern Notes
Yoke is worked from shoulders down to underarms and placed on holders; sleeves are worked from armhole to cuff; the body is then joined at underarm and worked in 1 piece to side-vent split, at which point back and fronts are worked separately.

Pat is worked back and forth; a circular needle is used to accommodate the large number of sts.

## Instructions
### Back Yoke
With larger needle, cast on 84 (92, 102, 110, 118, 126) sts.

Work in St st until piece measures 9½ (9¾, 10, 10¼, 10½, 11) inches from beg, ending with a WS row. Place all sts on holder or waste yarn.

### Front Yokes & Neck Shaping
With RS facing and using larger needle, pick up and knit 26 (29, 33, 36, 39, 42) sts along cast-on edge of back; skip center 32 (34, 36, 38, 40, 42) back neck sts, with 2nd ball of yarn, pick up and knit rem 26 (29, 33, 36, 39, 42) sts.

Working both sides at once with separate balls of yarn, work in St st and inc 1 st at each neck edge [every 4 rows] 7 (8, 9, 10, 11, 12) times, then [every 2 rows] 8 times. (41, 45, 50, 54, 58, 62 sts each side)

Work even until fronts measure same as back, ending with a WS row.

Place all sts on holder or waste yarn.

### Sleeves
With RS facing, using larger needle and beg at lower edge of yoke, pick up and knit 94 (100, 106, 112, 118, 124) sts along armhole edge. Do not join.

Purl 1 row.

Beg K4, P2 Rib and work 6 rows even.

**Dec row (RS):** K1, ssk, work in rib as established to last 3 sts, k2tog, k1.

Rep Dec row [every 6th row] 5 times. (82, 88, 94, 100, 106, 112 sts)

Work even until sleeve measures 5¾ (5¾, 6, 6, 6¼, 6½) inches, ending with WS row.

Work Beaded Edging pat. Bind off all sts loosely.

### Body
With WS facing, sl right front, back and left front sts to larger needle.

**Row 1 (RS):** *Knit across left front, cast on 3 (4, 5, 5, 6, 6) sts, place marker, cast on 3 (4, 5, 5, 6, 6) for underarm; rep from * across back; knit to end. (178, 198, 222, 238, 258, 274 sts)

Work 11 rows even in St st.

### Medium, Large, 2X-Large only
**Back Dec row (RS):** Slipping markers as you come to them, knit to first marker, k2tog, knit to 2 sts before next marker, k2tog, knit to end. (196, 220, 256 sts)

### All Sizes
Work even in St st until piece measures 4 inches from underarm, ending with a WS row.

Work even in Rib pat for 7 (7, 7¼, 7½, 7¾, 8) inches, ending with a WS row, and *at the same time*, on **small, extra-large, 3X-large only**, on last row, p2tog following each marker. (176, 196, 220, 236, 256, 272 sts)

## Left Front Vent

**Row 1 (RS):** Work 44 (49, 55, 59, 64, 68) sts of left front, place rem sts on holder or waste yarn.

**Row 2:** Sl 1 (side edge), work in rib as established to end.

**Row 3:** Work in rib to end.

Rep last 2 rows until piece measures 4¼ (4¼, 4½, 4¾, 5, 5¼) inches from division, or ¾ inch less than desired length, ending with a WS row.

Work Beaded Edging pat, working [k2tog, yo, ssk] in the K4 panels of the rib.

Bind off loosely.

## Back Vent

Sl 88 (98, 110, 118, 128, 136) back sts to larger needle.

**Row 1 (RS):** Sl 1, work in rib as established to end.

Rep Row 1 until piece measures same as left front to Beaded Edging pat.

Work Beaded Edging pat, working [k2tog, yo, ssk] in the K4 panels of the rib.

Bind off loosely.

## Right Front Vent

Sl rem sts to larger needle.

**Row 1 (RS):** Sl 1 (side edge), work in rib as established to end.

**Row 2:** Work in rib to end.

Finish as for left front.

## Front Edging

With RS facing and using smaller needle, pick up and knit 56 (57, 60, 61, 64, 65) sts along front to last row of neck shaping; 61 (62, 64, 65, 67, 68) sts to shoulder; 32 (34, 36, 38, 40, 42) sts across back neck; 61 (62, 64, 65, 67, 68) sts down left front to last row of neck shaping; and 56 (57, 60, 61, 64, 65) sts to bottom. (266, 272, 284, 290, 302, 308 sts)

**Row 1 (WS):** K2, [p4, 2] to end.

Work Beaded Edging pat, working [k2tog, yo, ssk] in the K4 panels of the rib.

Bind off loosely.

## Finishing

Weave in all ends. Sew underarm and sleeve seams. Block to finished measurements.

Sew buttons evenly spaced on left front; use facing yo's on right front for buttonholes. ▼

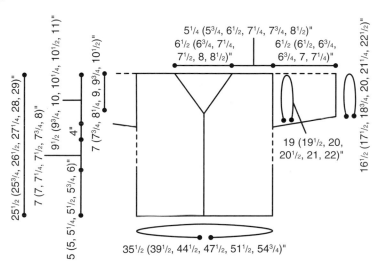

25½ (25¾, 26½, 27¼, 28, 29)"

7 (7, 7¼, 7½, 7¾, 8)"

9½ (9¾, 10, 10¼, 10½, 11)"

4"

7 (7¾, 8¼, 9, 9¾, 10½)"

5 (5, 5¼, 5½, 5¾, 6)"

5¼ (5¾, 6½, 7¼, 7¾, 8½)"

6½ (6¾, 7¼, 7½, 8, 8½)"

6½ (6½, 6¾, 6¾, 7, 7¼)"

19 (19½, 20, 20½, 21, 22)"

16½ (17½, 18¾, 20, 21¼, 22½)"

35½ (39½, 44½, 47½, 51½, 54¾)"

# oh baby chevron

Design by Debbie O'Neill

Combine a pretty chevron stitch with cotton yarn and elbow-length sleeves, and enjoy wearing this tunic any season of the year!

## Skill Level
■■■□ INTERMEDIATE

## Sizes
Woman's small (medium, large, extra-large, 2X-large, 3X-large) Instructions are given for smallest size, with larger sizes in parentheses. When only 1 number is given, it applies to all sizes.

## Finished Measurements
**Chest:** 34¾ (38½, 40, 44, 46½, 49½) inches
**Length:** 24½ (26, 27, 28, 30, 30) inches

## Materials
▼ Brown Sheep Cotton Fleece 80 percent pima cotton/20 percent wool medium weight yarn (215 yds/100g per skein): 4 (5, 5, 6, 7, 8) skeins new age teal #CW400
▼ Size 6 (4mm) double-pointed and 16-inch, 24-inch, 32-inch circular needles or size needed to obtain gauge
▼ Stitch markers, 1 in CC for beg of rnd
▼ Waste yarn or stitch holders
▼ Tapestry needle
▼ 2 (2, 2½, 2½, 3, 3) yards of ¼-inch wide satin ribbon

## Gauge
21 sts and 32 rows = 4 inches/10cm in St st
18 sts and 26 rows = 4 inches/10cm in Chevron Lace pat
To save time, take time to check gauge.

## Special Abbreviations
**Pm:** Place marker.
**M1 (Make 1):** Insert LH needle from front to back under horizontal strand between last st worked and next st, with RH needle, knit in back of lp.

## Pattern Stitch
**Chevron Lace** (multiple of 7 sts)
**Rnds 1 and 3:** Knit.
**Rnd 2:** *K1, k2tog, yo, k1, yo, ssk, k1; rep from * around.
**Rnd 4:** *K2tog, yo, k3, yo, ssk; rep from * around.
Rep Rnds 1–4 for pat.

## Pattern Notes

This garment is worked with raglan shaping, beg at back neck; when front neck and yoke are complete, the body is joined and worked to lower edge; the sleeves are worked in the rnd from the underarm to cuff.

Change to longer circular needle or dpns when sts no longer fit comfortably on the needle in use.

## Instructions
### Body

Using 24-inch circular needle, cast on 56 (60, 64, 68, 72, 76) sts. Do not join.

**Row 1 (WS):** Purl, placing markers as follows: 1 front st, pm, 1 raglan seam st, pm, 10 (11, 12, 13, 14, 15) sleeve sts, pm, 1 raglan seam st, pm, 30 (32, 34, 36, 38, 40) back sts, pm, 1 raglan seam st, pm, 10 (11, 12, 13, 14, 15) sleeve sts, pm, 1 raglan seam st, pm, 1 front st.

### Begin Raglan

**Inc Row 1 (RS):** *Knit to marker, yo, sl marker, k1, sl marker, yo; rep from * across, then knit to end. (64, 68, 72, 76, 80, 84 sts)

Continue in St st and rep Inc Row 1 [every other row] twice, ending with a WS row. (80, 84, 88, 92, 96, 100 sts)

### Shape Front Neck

**Inc Row 2 (RS):** K1, M1, *knit to marker, yo, sl marker, k1, sl marker, yo; rep from * across, then knit to last st, M1, k1. (90, 94, 98, 102, 106, 110 sts)

Rep Inc Row 2 [every other row] 12 (13, 14, 15, 16, 17) times, ending with a WS row. (210, 224, 238, 252, 266, 280 sts)

**Next row (RS):** Work Inc Row 1, then turn and with WS facing and using cable cast-on method (see page 10), cast on 2 sts. Turn back to RS, pm for beg of rnd and join. (220, 234, 248, 262, 276, 290 sts)

Continue in St st and rep Inc Rnd 1 [every other rnd] 9 (12, 13, 16, 17, 18) times, ending at first raglan marker following last inc rnd. (292, 330, 352, 390, 412, 434 sts)

### Separate Sections

Removing markers, sl next 64 (73, 78, 87, 92, 97) sts to waste yarn for sleeve, cast on 4 sts for underarm, pm for new beg of rnd, cast on 4 sts for underarm, knit across back sts, sl next 64 (73, 78, 87, 92, 97) sts to waste yarn for sleeve, cast on 8 sts for underarm, knit to end of rnd. (180, 200, 212, 232, 244, 256 sts)

### Body

**Rnd 1:** Knit inc 2 (inc 3, dec 2, dec 1, inc 1, inc 3) sts evenly spaced, preferably in underarm area. (182, 203, 210, 231, 245, 259 sts)

Work even in St st until body measures 4 (5, 6, 6½, 7, 7½) from underarm.

**Eyelet rnd:** [K9, k2tog, yo] 2 (3, 10, 11, 5, 11) times, [k8, k2tog, yo] 16 (17, 10, 11, 19, 5) times.

Work 5 rnds even in St st.

Beg Chevron Lace pat and work even for 13 (12½, 12, 11½, 12½, 11½) inches or desired length.

Bind off very loosely.

**Sleeves**
Sl the right sleeve sts to 16-inch circular needle.

With RS facing and beg at center underarm, pick up 4 sts from underarm, knit around sleeve, pick up 4 sts from underarm, pm for beg of rnd and join. (72, 81, 86, 95, 100, 105 sts)

Work even in St st for approx 1 (1, 1, 1, 1½, 1½) inches.

**Dec rnd:** K1, ssk, knit to 3 sts before end of rnd, k2tog, k1. (70, 79, 84, 93, 98, 103 sts)

Rep Dec rnd [every 4 rnds] 6 (8, 10, 13, 14, 14) times. (58, 63, 64, 67, 70, 75 sts)

Work even until sleeve measures 7 (7½, 8, 8½, 8½, 9) inches from underarm, or ½ inch less than desired length.

*Knit 1 rnd, purl 1 rnd; rep from * twice more.

Bind off all sts.

Rep for left sleeve.

**Finishing**
**Neck edging**
With RS facing and using 16-inch circular needle, pick up and knit approx 84 (88, 96, 104, 116, 124) sts around neck.

Purl 1 rnd, knit 1 rnd.

Bind off all sts purlwise. Weave in all ends. Block to finished measurements.

Beg at center front, weave ribbon in and out of eyelets. ▼

**OH BABY CHEVRON**

**STITCH KEY**
- ☐ Knit
- ☒ K2tog
- ○ Yo
- ☒ Ssk

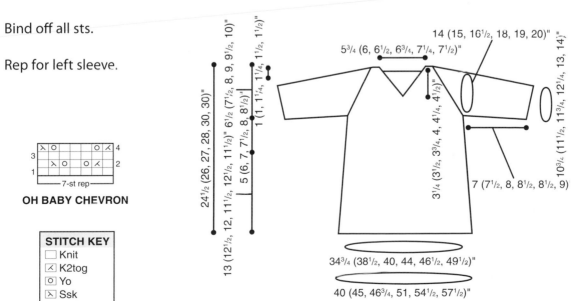

# soothing waves

Design by Joyce Nordstrom

The lacy yarn over patterning looks impressive, but the real plus is how quickly it comes off your needles!

## Skill Level
■■□□ EASY

## Sizes
Woman's small (medium, large, extra-large, 2X-large, 3X-large) Instructions are given for smallest size, with larger sizes in parentheses. When only 1 number is given, it applies to all sizes.

## Finished Measurements
**Chest:** 36 (40, 44, 48, 52, 56) inches
**Length:** 23½ (24½, 25½, 26½, 27½, 28½) inches

## Materials
▼ Plymouth Fantasy Naturale 100 percent cotton medium weight yarn (140 yds/100g per skein): 6 (6, 7, 7, 8, 8) skeins white #8001 (MC); 2 skeins natural #7650 (CC)
▼ Size 6 (4mm) 16- and 29-inch circular needles
▼ Size 8 (5mm) 29-inch circular needle or size needed to obtain gauge
▼ Stitch marker
▼ Stitch holders or waste yarn
▼ Tapestry needle

## Gauge
16 sts and 20 rows = 4 inches/10cm in St st with larger needle
To save time, take time to check gauge.

## Pattern Stitches
**A. Wavy Garter St** (multiple of 10 sts + 6)
**Rows 1 (RS) and 2:** Knit.
**Row 3:** K6, *[yo] twice, k1, [yo] 3 times, k1, [yo] 4 times, k1, [yo] 3 times, k1, [yo] twice, k6; rep from * across.
**Row 4:** Knit across, dropping all yo's.
**Rows 5 and 6:** Knit.
**Row 7:** K1, *[yo] twice, k1, [yo] 3 times, k1, [yo] 4 times, k1, [yo] 3 times, k1, [yo] twice, k6; rep from *, ending last rep k1 instead of k6.
**Row 8:** Knit across, dropping all yo's.
**B. Stripes**
4 rows MC, 4 rows CC, *8 rows MC, 4 rows CC; rep from *.

## Pattern Notes
The yoke is worked from shoulders down to underarms and placed on holders; the sleeves are worked down from the armhole; the body is then joined at the underarm and worked in 1 piece to bottom.

Pat is worked back and forth, except for neck edging; circular needles are used to accommodate the large number of sts.

## Instructions
### Back Yoke
With larger needle and MC, cast on 72 (80, 88, 96, 104, 112) sts.

Work even in St st until piece measures 9½ (10, 10½, 11, 11½, 12) inches, ending with a WS row.

Place all sts on waste yarn or holder.

### Front Yoke & Neck Shaping
With RS facing, using larger needle and MC, pick up and knit 22 (26, 29, 32, 35, 39) sts along cast-on edge of back; skip center 32 (34, 36, 38, 40, 42) back neck sts; with 2nd ball of MC, pick up and knit rem 22 (26, 29, 32, 35, 39) sts.

Working both sides at once with separate balls of yarn, work in St st and inc 1 st at each neck edge [every RS row] 7 times, ending with a WS row. (29, 33, 36, 39, 42, 46 sts each side)

**Next row (RS):** Knit across right front, cast on 14 (14, 16, 18, 20, 20) st for front neck, knit to end. (72, 80, 88, 96, 104, 112 sts)

Work even until front measures same as back, ending with a WS row.

Place all sts on waste yarn or holder.

### Sleeves
With RS facing, using larger needle and MC, and beg at lower edge, pick up and knit 76, (80, 84, 88, 94, 98) sts along armhole edge; do not join.

Purl 1 row.

**Dec row (RS):** K1, ssk, knit to last 3 sts, k2tog, k1. (84, 78, 82, 86, 92, 96 sts)

Continue in St st and rep Dec row [every other row] 3 (4, 7, 9, 10, 13) times, then [every 4th row] 15 (15, 14, 13, 12, 11) times. (38, 40, 40, 42, 46, 48 sts)

Work even until sleeve measures 14 (14½, 14½, 15, 15½, 16) inches from beg, or 1 inch short of desired length, ending with a WS row.

**Next row:** Change to smaller needle and rep Dec row. (36, 38, 38, 40, 44, 46 sts)

Knit 4 rows.

Bind off loosely.

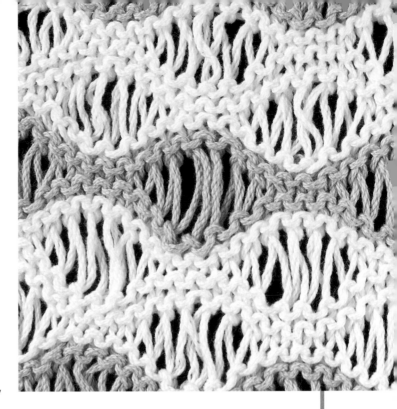

## Body

Transfer front and back sts to larger needle.

With RS facing and using MC, knit across; do not join.

### Small, Medium, Extra-Large, 2X-Large, 3X-Large only

**Next row (WS):** Purl and inc 2 (inc 6, inc 4, dec 2, inc 2) sts evenly across. (146, 166, 196, 206, 226 sts)

### Large only

**Next row (WS):** Purl. (176 sts)

Work even in Wavy Garter St and Stripe pat until body measures approx 13 (13½, 14, 14½, 15, 15½) inches or 1 inch short of desired length from underarm, ending with Row 4 or 8 of pat.

**Next row (RS):** Change to smaller needle and knit, dec 10 sts evenly spaced across.

Knit 4 rows.

Bind off loosely.

## Finishing

Sew side (matching pat) and sleeve seams.

## Neck edging

With RS facing and using smaller 16-inch needle and MC, pick up and knit 43 (45, 47, 49, 51, 53) sts around front neck and 30 (30, 32, 34, 36, 36) sts across back neck; place marker for beg of rnd. (73, 75, 79, 83, 87, 89 sts)

*Purl 1 rnd, knit 1 rnd; rep from * once more.

Bind off loosely. Weave in all loose ends. Block to finished measurements. ▼

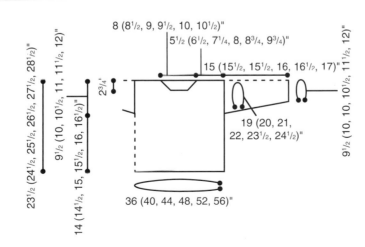

# harmony kimono

Design by Celeste Pinheiro

This appealing kimono features basket-weave borders and loose raglan sleeves.

## Skill Level

■■■□ INTERMEDIATE

## Sizes

Woman's extra-small (small, medium, large, extra-large, 2X-large) Instructions are given for smallest size, with larger sizes in parentheses. When only 1 number is given, it applies to all sizes.

## Finished Measurements

**Chest:** 36 (40½, 44, 47½, 52, 55½) inches, excluding front overlap
**Length:** 24 (24, 25, 26, 27, 29) inches

## Materials

- ▼ Plymouth Fantasy Naturale 100 percent cotton medium weight yarn (140 yds/100g per skein): 7 (7, 8, 9, 10, 11) skeins green #8011
- ▼ Size 6 (4mm) 29-inch (or longer) circular needle
- ▼ Size 8 (5mm) 29-inch (or longer) circular needle or size needed to obtain gauge
- ▼ Medium-sized crochet hook (to make buttonhole loop)
- ▼ 4 stitch markers
- ▼ Tapestry needle
- ▼ 1 large button or other closure (2 long beads used on sample)
- ▼ ¾-inch button for inside closure

## Gauge

18 sts and 24 rows = 4 inches/10cm in St st using larger needle
To save time, take time to check gauge.

## Special Abbreviations

**Pm:** Place marker
**M1 (Make 1):** Insert LH needle from front to back under horizontal strand between last st worked and next st, with RH needle, knit in back of lp.

## Pattern Stitch

**Basket Weave** (multiple of 8 sts + 1)
**Row 1 (RS):** Knit.
**Rows 2 and 4:** *P2, k5, p1; rep from * to last st, p1.
**Row 3:** *K2, p5, k1; rep from * to last st, k1.
**Row 5:** Knit.
**Row 6:** K3, p3, k2; rep from * to last st, k1.
**Row 7:** *P3, k3, p2; rep from * to last 1 st, p1.
**Row 8:** Rep Row 6.
Rep Rows 1–8 for pat.

## Pattern Notes

Pat is worked back and forth; circular needles are used to accommodate the large number of sts.

Read pat thoroughly before starting. Front and raglan shaping occur simultaneously, and front shaping continues after body is divided from sleeves.

Inc at neck edges by working M1 inc after first st and before last st.

Basket Weave pat may not work evenly into body st count—just work across until sts run out.

## Instructions
### Yoke
With larger needles, cast on 51 (51, 57, 67, 87, 95) sts.

**Set up raglan**
**Row 1 (WS):** Purl, placing markers as follows: 2 front sts, pm, 1 raglan seam st, pm, 5 (5, 7, 9, 17, 19) sleeve sts, pm, 1 raglan seam st, pm, 33 (33, 35, 41, 45, 49) back sts, pm, 1 raglan seam st, pm, 5 (5, 7, 9, 17, 19) sleeve sts, pm, 1 raglan seam st, pm, 2 front sts.

**Row 2 (RS):** *Knit to marker, yo, sl marker, k1, sl marker, yo; rep from * across, then knit to end. (59, 59, 65, 75, 95, 103 sts)

Continue in St st, working a yo before and after marked sts [every other row] 19 (24, 27, 27, 30, 32) more times and *at the same time,* inc 1 st at each neck edge [every 4th row] 11 (13, 14, 18, 19, 21) times, then [every other row] 13 (11, 13, 17, 17, 19) times.

Work 1 WS row following last raglan inc row.

### Divide for Sleeves & Body
**Next row (RS):** Work to first marker (right front), place next 47 (57, 65, 67, 81, 87) sts on holder (right sleeve), cast on 8 (8, 8, 10, 10, 10) sts (underarm), knit to next marker (back), place next 47 (57, 65, 67, 81, 87) sts on holder (left sleeve), cast on 8 (8, 8, 10, 10, 10) sts (underarm), work to end (left front).

### Body
Work in St st, continuing to work front inc until body measures approx 7¼ (5¾, 5¾, 6¾, 6¾, 7) inches from underarm, ending with a WS row.

**Next row:** Beg Basket Weave pat and continue working front edge inc as necessary.

*At the same time,* after front edge inc are complete—181 (201, 221, 247, 265, 285) sts— and following either Row 4 or 8 of Basket Weave pat, beg dec as follows:

**Dec row (Row 1 or 5 of pat):** K1, k2tog, work in pat as established to last 3 sts, ssk, k1. (179, 199, 219, 245, 263, 283 sts)

Rep Dec row [every 4th row] 10 (10, 10, 10, 10, 11) more times. (159, 179, 199, 225, 243, 261 sts)

Work even until body measures approx 17¼ (15¾, 15¾, 16¾, 16¾, 18) inches from underarm or desired length.

Bind off.

### Sleeve
With larger needle and beg at center underarm, pick up and knit 4 (4, 4, 5, 5, 5) sts from body underarm, k47 (57, 65, 67, 81, 87) sts from holder, pick up and knit 4 (4, 4, 5, 5, 5) sts from body underarm. (55, 65, 73, 77, 91, 97 sts)

Work even in St st until sleeve measures approx 8¼ (7¾, 5¾, 6¾, 6¾, 7) inches from underarm, ending with a WS row. (59, 67, 75, 83, 91, 99 sts)

**Next row (RS):** K1 (edge st), work Basket Weave pat to last st, and *at the same time,* inc 4 (2, 2, 6, 0, 2) evenly across, k1 (edge st). (59, 67, 75, 83, 91, 99 sts)

Work even until sleeve measures approx 13¼ (12¾, 11¾, 12¾, 11¾, 12) inches or desired length from underarm, ending with Row 4 or 8 of pat.

Bind off.

### Finishing
### Front band
With RS facing and using smaller needle, pick up approx 260 (260, 273, 285, 310, 318) sts evenly along fronts and back neck.

Knit 1 row.

Bind off. Sew sleeve seams. Block to finished measurements.

Make a braid with 3 strands about 20 inches long.

Fold in half and attach center of braid to corner of right front for tie.

Sew large button on left front aligned with tie.

With crochet hook, make a small lp using ch st and attach to corner of left front.

Sew small button opposite lp on WS of right front. ▼

**HARMONY KIMONO**

**STITCH KEY**
☐ K on RS, p on WS
⊟ P on RS, k on WS

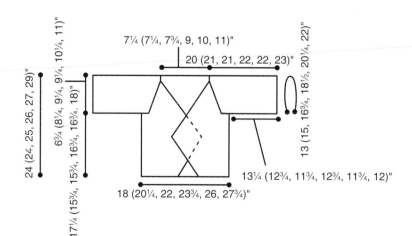

7¼ (7¼, 7¾, 9, 10, 11)"

20 (21, 21, 22, 22, 23)"

24 (24, 25, 26, 27, 29)"

6¾ (8¼, 9¼, 9¼, 10¼, 11)"

17¼ (15¾, 15¾, 16¾, 16¾, 18)"

13 (15, 16¾, 18½, 20¼, 22)"

13¼ (12¾, 11¾, 12¾, 11¾, 12)"

18 (20¼, 22, 23¾, 26, 27¾)"

# cellular t-top

Design by Nazanin S. Fard

This is the perfect sweater when you are interested in striking results in a hurry.

## Skill Level
 INTERMEDIATE

## Sizes
Woman's small (medium, large, extra-large, 2X-large, 3X-large) Instructions are given for smallest size, with larger sizes in parentheses. When only 1 number is given, it applies to all sizes.

## Finished Measurements
**Chest:** 29 (33½, 41½, 46½, 51¼, 56) inches
**Length:** 24¾ inches

## Materials
- TLC Cotton Plus 51 percent cotton/49 percent acrylic medium weight yarn (178 yds/100g per skein): 4 (5, 6, 7, 8, 9) skeins tangerine #3252
- Size 7 (4.5mm) 16- and two 29-inch circular needles
- Size 8 (5mm) 29-inch circular needle or size needed to obtain gauge
- Size H/8 (5mm) crochet hook or larger
- Waste yarn
- Stitch holders
- Stitch marker
- Tapestry needle

## Gauge
20 sts and 24 rows = 4 inches/10cm in St st with larger needle
20 sts and 24 rows = 4 inches/10cm in Cellular Lace pat with smaller needle
To save time, take time to check gauge.

## Special Techniques
**Provisional Cast On:** With crochet hook and waste yarn, make a chain several sts longer than desired cast on. With knitting needle and project yarn, pick up indicated number of sts in the "bumps" on back of chain. When indicated in pat, "unzip" the crochet chain to free live sts.

**3-Needle Bind Off:** With RS tog and needles parallel, using a 3rd needle, knit tog a st from the front needle with a st from the back needle. *Knit tog a st from the front and back needles, and sl the first st over the 2nd to bind off. Rep from * until number of sts indicated in pat are bound off, then continue as indicated.

**Lifted Increase:** At end of row, k1, k1 2 rows below last st worked; at beg of row, k1 in row below next st, k1.

## Pattern Stitches
**A. Cellular Lace** (multiple of 4 sts + 2)

**Row 1 (RS):** K1, *k2tog, yo, ssk; rep from * to last st, k1.
**Row 2:** P2, *(p1, p1-tbl) in yo, p2; rep from * to end.
**Row 3:** K1, yo, *ssk, k2tog, yo; rep from * to last st, k1.
**Row 4:** P4, *(p1, p1-tbl) in yo, p2; rep from * to last 2 sts, p2.
Rep Rows 1–4 for pat.
**B. Garter St** (in the rnd)
**Rnd 1:** Knit.
**Rnd 2:** Purl.
Rep Rnds 1 and 2 for pat.

### Pattern Notes
Pat is worked back and forth on a circular needle until front and back are joined, at which point it is worked in the rnd.

The st count decreases on Rows 1 and 3 of pat; count your sts following Rows 2 and 4 only.

### Instructions
### Back
With smaller needle and using the provisional method, cast on 122 (134, 154, 166, 178, 190) sts.

Purl 1 row.

Work even in Cellular Lace until piece measures 10 inches.

Sl sts to holder, do not cut yarn.

### Front
Unzip crochet chain of provisional cast on for first 44 (48, 60, 64, 68, 72) sts from the RH side of back sts; unzip next 34 (38, 34, 38, 42, 46) sts and put on holder for back neck; unzip rem 44 (48, 60, 64, 68, 72) sts and sl to needle.

Beg with RS facing and working both sides at once with separate balls of yarn, knit 11 rows.

**Next row (WS):** Purl.

**Neck Inc row (RS):** Work in Cellular Lace pat to 2 sts before neck, work lifted inc in next st, k1; k1, work lifted inc in next st, work in Cellular Lace pat to end. (45, 49, 61, 65, 69, 73 sts each side)

Rep Inc row [every other row] 8 (9, 8, 8, 8, 9) times, working new sts in pat as established as they accumulate. (53, 58, 69, 73, 77, 82 sts each side)

**Neck joining row (WS):** Work left front, cast on 16 (18, 16, 20, 24, 26) sts, then continue to work right front with same yarn, cutting yarn for right front.

Work even until piece measures 10 inches, ending on same row as back.

### Join front & back
Sl back sts to 2nd smaller needle.

Join sleeve underarm seams

Turn WS out.

**Row 1:** Using 3-Needle Bind Off, bind off 25 sts for underarm sleeve seam, then purl the back sts, turn.

**Row 2:** Using 3-Needle Bind Off, bind off 25 sts for underarm sleeve seam, then purl the front sts. (144, 168, 208, 232, 256, 280 sts)

### Body
Turn RS out, change to larger needle, and beg working in the rnd, placing marker at beg of rnd.

Work even in St st until piece measures 14 inches or desired length from underarm.

Change to smaller needle and work 8 rnds of Garter St.

Bind off all sts loosely.

### Finishing
Neck edge
Sl 34 (38, 34, 38, 42, 46) back neck sts to smaller needle, then pick up and knit 9 (10, 9, 9, 9, 10) sts along side of front neck, 16 (18, 16, 20, 24, 26) sts in center front neck and 9 (10, 9, 9, 9, 10) sts along other side of front

neck; place marker for beg of rnd and join. (68, 76, 68, 76, 84, 92 sts)

Work 6 rnds of garter st.

Bind off all sts loosely.

Sleeve edge
With smaller 16-inch needle, pick up and knit and 68 sts around sleeve edge.

Work 10 rnds of garter st.

Bind off all sts loosely. Weave in all ends. Block to finished measurements. ▼

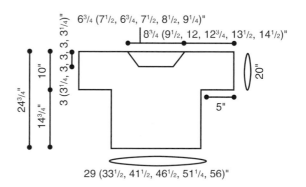

# gentle lace

**Design by Celeste Pinheiro**

If you haven't tried lace knitting before, this is your lucky day! This simple cloverleaf pattern has just a six-row repeat.

## Skill Level
◼◼◻◻ EASY

## Sizes
Woman's small (medium, large, extra-large, 2X-large) Instructions are given for smallest size, with larger sizes in parentheses. When only 1 number is given, it applies to all sizes.

## Finished Measurements
**Chest:** 36 (40¾, 44, 48¾, 52) inches (buttoned)
**Length:** 23½ (24½, 25½, 26½, 27¼) inches

## Materials
▼ Reynolds Top Seed Cotton 100 percent mercerized cotton light weight yarn (105 yds/50g per hank): 8 (9, 10, 11, 12) hanks taupe #406
▼ Size 4 (3.5mm) 16- and 29-inch circular needles
▼ Size 6 (4mm) 16- and 29-inch circular needles or size needed to obtain gauge
▼ Stitch markers
▼ Waste yarn
▼ Tapestry needle
▼ 3 (½-inch) buttons (or desired number)

## Gauge
21 sts and 25 rows = 4 inches/10cm in St st using larger needle
To save time, take time to check gauge.

## Special Abbreviations
**Pm:** Place marker.
**Sm:** Slip marker.

## Special Technique
**I-Cord:** *K3, do not turn, sl sts back to LH needle; rep from * until cord is desired length. Bind off.

## Pattern Stitch
**Cloverleaf Lace** (multiple of 6 sts + 1)
**Row 1 (RS):** P1, *k1, yo, sk2p, yo, k1, p1; rep from * to end.
**Row 2 (and all WS rows):** Purl.
**Row 3:** P1, *k2, yo, ssk, k1, p1; rep from * to end.
**Row 5:** P1, *k5, p1; rep from * to end.
**Row 6:** Rep Row 2.
Rep Rows 1–6 for pat.

## Pattern Notes
The raglan yoke is worked first, then sts are

separated; body is joined and worked down to bottom edge; sleeves are worked down from yoke.

The body is worked back and forth; a circular needle is used to accommodate the large number of sts; the sleeve is worked in the rnd.

Front neck and raglan shaping occur simultaneously, and front neck shaping continues after body is divided from sleeves.

A chart for the Cloverleaf Lace pat is included for those preferring to work from charts.

## Instructions
### Yoke
With larger needle, cast on 79 (77, 81, 79, 85) sts.

**Raglan set-up row (WS):** Purl across, placing markers as follows: 2 front sts, pm, 1 raglan seam st, pm, 16 (14, 14, 12, 12) sleeve sts, pm, 1 raglan seam st, pm, 39 (41, 45, 49, 53) back sts, pm, 1 raglan seam st, pm, 16 (14, 14, 12, 12) sleeve sts, pm, 1 raglan seam st, pm, 2 front sts.

**Raglan Inc row (RS):** *Knit to marker, yo, sm, k1, sm, yo; rep from *, then knit to end. (87, 85, 89, 87, 93 sts)

Continue in St st, working yo inc each side of marked raglan seam sts [every other row] 21 (25, 28, 30, 32) times and *at the same time,* inc 1 st at each neck edge [every 4th row] 9 (10, 10, 11, 12) times, and [every other row] 9 (11, 12, 13, 15) times as follows: k1, k1 in row below next st, knit next st, work to last st, k1 2 rows below last st worked, k1.

Work 1 WS row following last Raglan Inc row.

### Divide for body & sleeves
**Next row (RS):** Work to first marker, sl next 62 (66, 72, 88, 82) sts to waste yarn

for sleeve, cast on 12 (12, 12, 16, 16) sts for underarm, knit to next marker, sl next 62 (66, 72, 88, 82) sts to waste yarn for sleeve, cast on 12 (12, 12, 16, 16) sts for underarm, work to end.

### Body
Continue in St st and complete neck inc. (187, 211, 229, 253, 271 sts)

Work even until piece measures 6 (5¾, 4¾, 5, 4¼) inches from underarm, ending with a WS row.

**Next row (RS):** Beg Cloverleaf Lace pat.

Work even until piece measures approx 16 (15¾, 15¾, 16, 16¼) inches from underarm, ending with Row 4.

**Next row (RS):** Change to smaller needle and knit 4 rows.

**Next row (RS):** K1, *k2tog, yo; rep from * to last 2 sts, k2.

Knit 1 row.

Bind off loosely.

## Sleeves

With RS facing, using larger 16-inch needle and beg at center underarm, pick up and knit 6 (6, 6, 8, 8) sts, knit across sts from holder, pick up and knit 6 (6, 6, 8, 8) sts, pm and join. (74, 78, 84, 90, 94 sts)

Knit 6 rnds.

Change to smaller needle.

Purl 1 rnd, knit 1 rnd, purl 1 rnd.

**Next rnd:** *K2tog, yo; rep from * around.

Purl 1 rnd.

Bind off loosely.

## Finishing

Block to finished measurements. Weave in all ends.

## Front Edging

With RS facing and using smaller needle, pick up and knit approx 368 (378, 388, 398, 408) sts evenly around fronts and back neck; exact st count isn't critical, but it must be an even number of sts.

Knit 3 rows.

**Next row (RS):** K1, *k2tog, yo; rep from * to last st, k1.

Knit 1 row.

Bind off.

## Tie

With smaller needle, cast on 3 sts.

Work I-Cord until it measures desired waist measurement plus 30 inches.

Thread through eyelets at top of Cloverleaf Lace pat.

Sew buttons evenly spaced as desired along left front edge, using opposite eyelet for buttonhole. ▼

**GENTLE LACE**

**STITCH KEY**
- ⊟ P on RS, k on WS
- ☐ K on RS, p on WS
- ⊙ Yo
- ⋏ Sk2p
- ⊠ Ssk

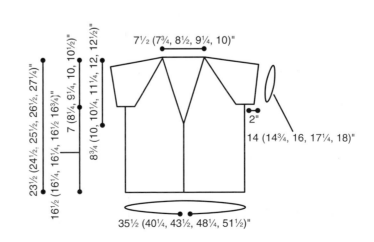

7½ (7¾, 8½, 9¼, 10)"

23½ (24½, 25½, 26½, 27¼)"

16½ (16¼, 16¼, 16½ 16¾)"

7 (8¼, 9¼, 10, 10½)"

8¾ (10, 10¼, 11¼, 12, 12½)"

2"

14 (14¾, 16, 17¼, 18)"

35½ (40¼, 43½, 48¼, 51½)"

# summer breeze top

**Design by Amy Polcyn**

There's just one circular piece to knit for this quick, comfortable and easy sweater.

### Skill Level
 **EASY**

### Sizes
Woman's small (medium, large, extra-large, 2X-large, 3X-large) Instructions are given for smallest size, with larger sizes in parentheses. When only 1 number is given, it applies to all sizes.

### Finished Measurements
**Chest:** 36 (40, 44, 48, 52, 56) inches
**Length (with collar folded):** 16 (16¾, 17½, 18¼, 19, 19¾) inches

### Materials
▼ Berroco Comfort 50 percent super-fine nylon/50 percent super-fine acrylic medium weight yarn (210 yds/100g per ball): 3 (4, 4, 5, 5, 6) balls rosebud #9723
▼ Size 8 (5mm) 24-inch circular needle or size needed to obtain gauge
▼ Spare needle 1 or 2 sizes larger (optional)
▼ Stitch markers
▼ Tapestry needle

### Gauge
20 sts and 28 rows = 4 inches/10cm in rib pat (slightly stretched)
To save time, take time to check gauge.

rnd and join, being careful not to twist sts. (216, 240, 264, 288, 312, 336 sts)

Work in K2, P2 Rib until piece measures 8 (8½, 9, 9½, 10, 10½) inches or desired length.

## Armholes
**Next rnd:** Removing markers, work in pat to 18 (20, 22, 24, 26, 28) sts before first marker, bind off next 36 (40, 44, 48, 52, 56) sts very loosely in pat, work in pat to 18 (20, 22, 24, 26, 28) sts before 2nd marker, bind off next 36 (40, 44, 48, 52, 56) sts.

**Next rnd:** Work in pat to first set of bound-off sts; with WS facing and using cable method, cast on 18 (20, 22, 24, 26, 28) sts above sts just bound off; work in pat to 2nd set of bound-off sts and rep cast on for other armhole; place marker for beg of rnd. (180, 200, 220, 240, 260, 280 sts)

## Body
Continue in rib as established for 12 (12½, 13, 13½, 14, 14½) inches or desired length.

Bind off very loosely in rib.

## Finishing
Weave in ends being careful to weave in any ends in top half on collar on the RS (they will be hidden when collar is folded down).

Fold down collar to match cast-on edge to armhole edge or desired depth. ▼

## Pattern Stitch
**K2, P2 Rib** (multiple of 4 sts)
**Rnd 1:** *K1, p2; rep from * around.
Rep Rnd 1 for pat.

## Pattern Notes
This top is worked in 1 piece in the rnd.

The ribbed fabric is very elastic and will fit bust size approx 2 inches smaller or larger than finished measurement.

When using cable cast on (see page 10) at underarm, turn work to WS before casting on.

Bind off very loosely, using a larger needle if necessary.

## Top
### Collar
Using cable method, cast on 108 (120, 132, 144, 156, 168), place marker, cast on 108 (120, 132, 144, 156, 168), place marker for beg of

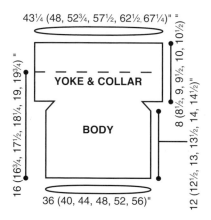

43¼ (48, 53¾, 57½, 62½, 67¼)" =

16 (16¾, 17½, 18¼, 19, 19¾) "

**YOKE & COLLAR**

**BODY**

8 (8½, 9, 9½, 10, 10½)"

12 (12½, 13, 13½, 14, 14½)"

36 (40, 44, 48, 52, 56)"

# awesome cables

Design by Susan Robicheau

Knit a cable sweater that will wow them! This comfy extra-long style has cables in front, in back and down the sleeves.

## Skill Level
■■■□ INTERMEDIATE

## Sizes
Woman's small (medium, large, extra large, 2X-large) Instructions are given for smallest size, with larger sizes in parentheses. When only 1 number is given, it applies to all sizes.

## Finished Measurements
**Chest:** 38 (42, 46, 50, 54) inches
**Length:** 25 (25½, 26½, 27, 27) inches

## Materials
▼ Plymouth Yarn Suri Merino 55 percent Suri alpaca/45 percent extra-fine merino wool medium weight yarn (109 yds/50g per ball): 11 (14, 17, 20, 23) balls periwinkle #1742
▼ Size 4 (3.5mm) double-pointed, 16- and 36-inch circular needles
▼ Size 6 (4mm) double-pointed, 16- and 36-inch circular needles or size needed to obtain gauge
▼ Size I/9 (5.5mm) crochet hook
▼ Waste yarn
▼ Stitch holder (optional)

▼ Cable needle
▼ Stitch markers, 2 in CCs for side seam and beg of rnd
▼ Stitch holders (optional)
▼ Tapestry needle

MEDIUM 4

## Gauge
20 sts and 28 rows = 4 inches/10cm St st with larger needle
To save time, take time to check gauge.

## Special Abbreviations
**C3B (Cable 3 Back):** Sl 1 to cn and hold to back of work, k2, k1 from cn.
**C3F (Cable 3 Front):** Sl 2 to cn and hold to front of work, k1, k2 from cn.
**C4B (Cable 4 Back):** Sl 2 to cn and hold to back of work, k2, k2 from cn.
**C4F (Cable 4 Front):** Sl 2 to cn and hold to front of work, k2, k2 from cn.
**C5B (Cable 5 Back):** Sl 3 to cn and hold to back of work, k2, k3 from cn.
**M1 (Make 1):** Insert LH needle from front to back under horizontal strand between last st worked and next st, with RH needle, knit in back of lp.

## Special Technique
**Provisional Cast On:** With crochet hook and waste yarn, make a chain several sts longer than desired cast on. With knitting needle and project yarn, pick up indicated number of sts in the "bumps" on back of chain. When indicated in pat, "unzip" the crochet chain to free live sts.

## Pattern Stitches
**A. Cable A** (9-st panel)
**Row 1 (RS):** C4B, k1, C4F.
**Row 2 (and all WS rows):** Purl.
**Row 3:** Knit.
**Row 5:** C4F, k1, C4B.
**Row 7:** K2, C5B, k2.
**Row 8:** Rep Row 2.
Rep Rows 1–8 for pat.
***Note:*** *When working pat in the rnd, knit every other rnd.*
**B. Cable B** (27 st panel)
**Row 1:** K5, C3B, k1, C4B, k1, C4F, k1, C3F, k5.
**Row 2 (and all WS rows):** P27.
**Row 3:** K4, C3B, k2tog, yo, k9, yo, ssk, C3F, k4.
**Row 5:** K3, C3B, k2tog, yo, k1, C4F, k1, C4B, k1, yo, ssk, C3F, k3.
**Row 7:** K2, C3B, [k2tog, yo] twice, k2, C5B, k2, [yo, ssk] twice, C3F, k2.

**Row 9:** K1, C3B, [k2tog, yo] twice, k1, C4B, k1, C4F, k1, [yo, ssk] twice, C3F, k1.
**Row 11:** C3B, [k2tog, yo] 3 times, k9, [yo, ssk] 3 times, C3F.
**Row 13:** C3F, k1, [k2tog, yo] twice, k1, C4F, k1, C4B, k1, [yo, ssk] twice, k1, C3B.
**Row 15:** K1, C3F, k1, [k2tog, yo] twice, k2, C5B, k2, [yo, ssk] twice, k1, C3B, k1.
**Row 17:** K2, C3F, k1, k2tog, yo, k1, C4B, k1, C4F, k1, yo, ssk, C3B, k2.
**Row 19:** K3, C3F, k1, k2tog, yo, k9, yo, ssk, k1, C3B, k3.
**Row 21:** K4, C3F, k2, C4F, k1, C4B, k2, C3B, k4.
**Row 23:** K5, C3F, k3, C5B, k3, C3B, k5.
**Row 24:** Rep Row 2.
Rep Rows 1–24 for pat.
***Note:*** *When working pat in the rnd, knit every other rnd.*

## Pattern Notes
The sweater begins at the top back yoke and is worked back and forth to the underarm; shoulder sts are picked up for the front yoke and worked to front underarm, after which the body is joined and worked in the rnd; the sleeves are worked in the rnd from the underarm.

Back and front yokes are worked back and forth; a circular needle is used to accommodate the large number of sts.

When working sleeves, change to dpns when sts no longer fit comfortably on circular needle.

Charts for the cable pats are included for those preferring to work from charts.

## Instructions
**Back Yoke**
With larger needle and using provisional method, cast on 95 (105, 115, 125, 135) sts.

**Row 1 (and all WS rows):** Purl.

**Pat set-up row (RS):** K10 (11, 13, 15, 16), *place marker, work Cable A across next 9 sts, place

marker, k24 (29, 31, 34, 38); rep from * once, place marker, work Cable A across next 9 sts, place marker, k10 (11, 13, 15, 16).

Work even in pat as established until piece measures approx 9 (9½, 10, 10½, 11) inches, ending with a WS row.

Sl sts to waste yarn or holder.

### Front Neck & Yoke
Unzip crochet chain of provisional cast on for first 29 (32, 35, 38, 40) back sts and sl sts to larger needle; unzip next 37 (41, 45, 49, 55) sts and sl to waste yarn or holder for back neck; unzip rem 29 (32, 35, 38, 40) back sts and sl to same larger needle.

Work both sides of neck at once with separate balls of yarn.

**Row 1 (and all WS rows):** Purl.

**Set up pat (RS):** K10 (11, 13, 15, 16), place marker, work Cable A over next 9 sts, place marker, k9 (11, 12, 13, 14), M1, k1; k1, M1, k9 (11, 12, 13, 14), place marker, work Cable A over next 9 sts, place marker, k10 (11, 13, 14, 16). (30, 33, 36, 39, 41 sts each side)

Continue to work pat as established, working

M1-inc 1 st in from neck edge [every other row] 6 (5, 10, 11, 9) times, then [every row] 2 (4, 0, 0, 4) time(s), ending with Row 7 of Cable A. (38, 42, 46, 50, 54 sts each side)

**Next row (WS):** P38 (42, 46, 50, 54), cast on 19 (21, 23, 25, 27) sts for front neck, p38 (42, 46, 50, 54). (95, 105, 115, 125, 135 sts)

**Set up center cable pat (RS):** Slipping markers as you come to them, knit to first marker, work Cable A, k15 (19, 22, 25, 29), place marker, work Cable B over next 27 sts, place marker, k15 (19, 22, 25, 29), work Cable A, knit to end.

Work even in pat as established until piece measures same as back, ending on same WS row as for back.

### Body
**Rnd 1:** With RS facing, work in pat across front, place CC1 marker for side, work across back sts from holder, place CC2 marker for side and beg of rnd, then join. (190, 210, 230, 250, 270 sts)

Work 20 rnds even.

**Dec rnd:** K1, k2tog, work to 3 sts before side marker, ssk, k1; rep from * once more. (186, 206, 226, 246, 266 sts)

Work 20 rnds even, then rep Dec rnd. (182, 202, 222, 242, 262 sts)

Work 20 rnds even.

**Inc rnd:** *K1, M1, work to 1 st before side marker, M1, k1; rep from * once more. (186, 206, 226, 246, 266 sts)

Work 20 rnds even then rep Inc rnd. (190, 210, 230, 250, 270 sts)

Work even in until piece measures approx 14 (13½, 14, 13½, 13) inches or 2 (2½, 2½, 3, 3) inches short of desired length, ending on

Row 12 or 24 and dec 1 st at each side on last rnd. (188, 208, 228, 248, 268 sts)

## Ribbing
Change to smaller needle.

Work even in K2, P2 rib for 2 (2½, 2½, 3, 3) inches.

Bind off very loosely in rib.

## Sleeves
With RS facing, using larger 16-inch needle and beg at underarm, pick up and knit 91 (95, 101, 105, 111) sts evenly spaced around armhole; place CC marker for beg of rnd and join.

**Dec rnd:** K1, k2tog, knit to last 3 sts, ssk, k1. (89, 93, 99, 103, 109 sts)

**Set up cable pat:** K40 (41, 45, 47, 50), place marker, work Cable A over next 9 sts, place marker, k40 (41, 45, 47, 50).

Continue in pat as established and *at the same time*, work Dec rnd [every 4th rnd] 25 (25, 26, 26, 26) times, changing to dpns when sts no longer fit comfortably on circular needle. (39, 43, 47, 51, 57 sts)

Work even until sleeve measures 15 inches or 2 (2, 2½, 2½, 3) inches short of desired length, and inc 1 (inc 1, inc 1, inc 1, dec 1) st on last rnd. (40, 44, 48, 52, 56 sts)

## Cuff
Change to smaller dpns and work K2, P2 rib for 2 (2, 2½, 2½, 3) inches.

Bind off very loosely in rib.

## Finishing
### Neckband
With RS facing and using smaller 16-inch needle, knit 37 (41, 45, 49, 55) back neck sts from holder, pick up and knit 12 (13, 15, 17,

19) sts along left neck edge, 19 (21, 23, 25, 27) front neck sts, 12 (13, 18, 17, 18) sts along right neck edge. (80, 88, 104, 108, 120 sts)

Work in K2, P2 rib for 1½ inches.

Bind off very loosely in rib. Weave in all ends. Block to finished measurements. ▼

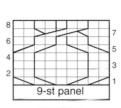

STITCH KEY
☐ K on RS, p on WS
◻ C3B
◻ C4B
◻ C4F
◻ C3F
☑ K2tog
⊙ Yo
◺ Ssk
◻ C5B

9-st panel

**CHART A**

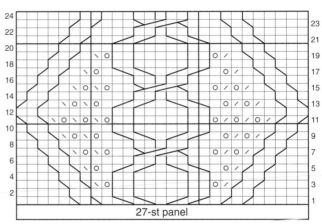

27-st panel

**CHART B**

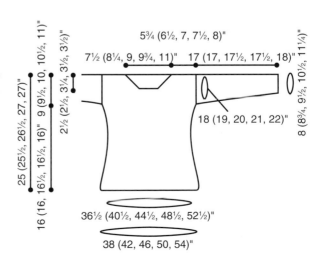

5¾ (6½, 7, 7½, 8)"

7½ (8¼, 9, 9¾, 11)"   17 (17, 17½, 17½, 18)"

25 (25½, 26½, 27, 27)"

16 (16, 16½, 16½, 16)"

9 (9½, 10, 10½, 11)"

2½ (2½, 3¼, 3½, 3½)"

18 (19, 20, 21, 22)"

8 (8¾, 9½, 10½, 11¼)"

36½ (40½, 44½, 48½, 52½)"

38 (42, 46, 50, 54)"

# cable & rib comfort

Design by Andra Knight-Bowman

This sweater proves that an interesting cable feature doesn't need to be difficult.

## Skill Level
■■■□ INTERMEDIATE

## Sizes
Woman's small (medium, large, extra-large, 2X-large) Instructions are given for smallest size, with larger sizes in parentheses. When only 1 number is given, it applies to all sizes.

## Finished Measurements
**Chest:** 36 (40, 44, 48, 52) inches
**Length:** 20 (21, 22, 23, 24) inches

## Materials
▼ Berroco Comfort 50 percent super-fine nylon/50 percent super-fine acrylic medium weight yarn (210 yds/100g per ball): 6 (7, 8, 9, 10) balls pumpkin #9724
▼ Size 5 (3.75mm) 16-inch circular needle
▼ Size 7 (4.5mm) double-point and 16-, 24-inch circular needles or size needed to obtain gauge
▼ Size H/8 (5mm) crochet hook (or larger)
▼ Waste yarn
▼ Stitch holder (optional)
▼ Stitch markers, 1 in CC for beg of rnd
▼ Cable needle
▼ Tapestry needle

## Gauge
20 sts and 25 rows = 4 inches/10cm in St st with larger needle
To save time, take time to check gauge.

## Special Abbreviations
**C4F (Cable 4 Front):** Sl 2 to cn and hold in front, k2, k2 from cn.
**Tw3B (Twist 3 Back):** Sl 1 to cn and hold in back, k2, p1 from cn.
**Tw3F (Twist 3 Front):** Sl 2 to cn and hold in front, p1, k2 from cn.
**M1 (Make 1):** Insert LH needle from front to back under horizontal strand between last st worked and next st, with RH needle, knit in back of lp.

## Special Technique
**Provisional Cast On:** With crochet hook and waste yarn, make a chain several sts longer than desired cast on. With knitting needle and project yarn, pick up indicated number of sts in the "bumps" on back of chain. When indicated in pat, "unzip" the crochet chain to free live sts.

## Pattern Stitch
**Diamond Cable** (20-st panel)
**Rnds 1, 2 and 4:** P8, k4, p8.

**Rnd 3:** P8, C4F, p8.
**Rnd 5:** P7, Tw3B, Tw3F, p7.
**Rnd 6:** P7, k2, p2, k2, p7.
**Rnd 7:** P6, Tw3B, p2, Tw3F, p6.
**Rnd 8:** P6, k2, p4, k2, p6.
**Rnd 9:** P5, Tw3B, p4, Tw3F, p5.
**Rnds 10–12:** P5, k2, p6, k2, p5.
**Rnd 13:** P5, Tw3F, p4, Tw3B, p5.
**Rnd 14:** Rep Rnd 8.
**Rnd 15:** P6, Tw3F, p2, Tw3B, p6.
**Rnd 16:** Rep Rnd 6.
**Rnd 17:** P7, Tw3F, Tw3B, p7.
**Rnd 18:** Rep Rnd 1.
**Rnd 19:** Rep Rnd 3.
**Rnd 20:** Rep Rnd 1.
Rep Rnds 1–20 for pat.

### Pattern Notes
The sweater begins at the top back yoke and is worked back and forth to the underarm; shoulder sts are picked up for the front yoke and worked to front underarm, after which the body is joined and worked in the rnd; the sleeves are worked in the rnd from the underarm.

Change to dpns when sts no longer fit comfortably on circular needle.

A chart for the Diamond Cable pat is included for those preferring to work from charts.

### Instructions
### Back Yoke
With larger needle and using provisional method, cast on 90 (100, 110, 120, 130) sts.

Work even in St st until piece measures 7½ (8, 8½, 9, 9½) inches, ending with a WS row.

Purl 1 row, knit 1 row.

Place sts on waste yarn or holder.

### Front Neck & Yoke
Unzip crochet chain of provisional cast on for first 29 (32, 36, 40, 45) back sts and sl sts to larger needle; unzip next 32 (36, 38, 40, 40) sts and put on holder for back neck; unzip rem 29 (32, 36, 40, 45) back sts and sl to same larger needle.

Work both sides at once with separate balls of yarn.

**Row 1 (RS):** Knit to 1 st before neck, M1, k1; k1, M1, knit to end. (30, 33, 37, 41, 45 sts each side)

**Row 2:** Purl.

Rep [Rows 1 and 2] 7 times. (37, 40, 44, 48, 53 sts each side)

**Next row:** K37 (40, 44, 48, 53), cast on 16 (20, 22, 24, 24) sts for front neck, then using same yarn and cutting other strand, k37 (40, 44, 48, 53). (90, 100, 110, 120, 130 sts)

Work even in St st until front measures same as back from shoulder, ending with a WS row.

Purl 1 row, knit 1 row.

## Body
### Sizes Small, Large, 2X-Large only
**Rnd 1:** With RS facing, k1, M1, knit to last st of front, M1, k1, work across back sts from holder, place CC marker for beg of rnd, join. (182, 222, 262 sts)

### Sizes Medium, X-Large only
**Rnd 1:** With RS facing, knit across front sts, sl back sts from holder to needle, k2tog, knit to last 2 sts, k2tog, place CC marker for beg of rnd, then join. (198, 238 sts)

### All Sizes
**Rnd 2 (set-up rnd):** K0 (0, 2, 2, 0), *p2, k2; rep from * 8 (9, 10, 11, 13) times, place marker, work Diamond Cable pat over next 20 sts, place marker, *k2, p2; rep from * to last 2 (2, 0, 0, 2) sts, end k2 (2, 0, 0, 2).

Work even in pat as established until body measures approx 12½ (13, 13½, 14, 14½) inches or desired length from underarm, ending on Rnd 1 or 11 of Cable pat.

Bind off very loosely in pat.

## Sleeves
With larger 16-inch circular needle, beg at underarm, pick up and knit 84 (88, 92, 96, 100) sts evenly around, place marker for beg of rnd and join.

Work 6 rnds of k2, p2 rib.

**Dec rnd:** Maintaining pat as established, dec 1 st before and after marker (either k2tog or p2tog as required by pat). (82, 86, 90, 94, 98 sts)

Rep Dec rnd [every 6th rnd] 17 times. (48, 52, 56, 60, 64 sts)

Work even until sleeve measures 17½ (18, 18, 18, 18) inches or desired length.

Bind off loosely in pat.

## Neck
With smaller 16-inch circular needle, pick up and knit 80 (84, 88, 92, 96) sts around neck, including back-neck sts on holder; place marker for beg of rnd and join.

Work k2, p2 rib for 2¼ inches.

Bind off loosely in pat, leaving a 20-inch tail.

Fold bound-off edge inside, then whipstitch to inside of pick-up rnd.

## Finishing
Weave in all ends. Block to finished measurements. ▼

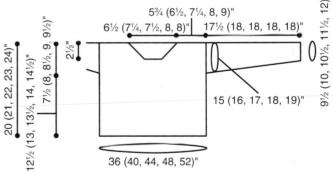

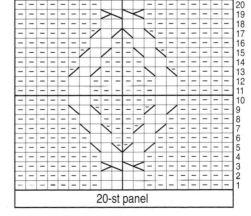

**STITCH KEY**
- ⊟ Purl
- ☐ Knit
- ⋈ C4F
- ⟋ Tw3B
- ⟍ Tw3F

20-st panel

**CABLE AND RIB COMFORT**

# warm woven jacket

Design by Nazanin S. Fard

The texture and updated classic styling will please everyone from size small to 2X. Try it on as you go to check the fit.

## Skill Level
 INTERMEDIATE

## Sizes
Woman's small (medium, large, extra-large, 2X-large) Instructions are given for smallest size, with larger sizes in parentheses. When only 1 number is given, it applies to all sizes.

## Finished Measurements
**Chest:** 37 (41, 45, 49, 53) inches (buttoned)
**Length:** 27 inches

## Materials
▼ Lion Brand Lion Wool 100 percent wool medium weight yarn (158 yd/85g per ball): 9 (10, 12, 13, 14) balls cadet blue #110
▼ Size 7 (4.5mm) 29-inch circular needle
▼ Size 8 (5mm) 29-inch circular needle or size needed to obtain gauge
▼ Size H/8 (5mm) crochet hook (or larger)
▼ Stitch holders
▼ Waste yarn
▼ 7 (¾-inch) buttons (shown with JHB International #45152)
▼ Tapestry needle

## Gauge
20 sts and 22 rows = 4 inches/10cm in Woven St with larger needle
To save time, take time to check gauge.

## Special Techniques
**Provisional Cast On:** With crochet hook and waste yarn, make a chain several sts longer than desired cast on. With knitting needle and project yarn, pick up indicated number of sts in the "bumps" on back of chain. When indicated in pat, "unzip" the crochet chain and sl live sts to needle or holder as necessary.

**1-Row Buttonhole:** Bind off next st by slipping next 2 sts to RH needle, then passing 2nd st on RH needle over first st; sl next st on LH needle to RH needle and pass 2nd st over as before. Sl rem st back to LH needle. Make double yo above bound-off sts.

## Pattern Stitch
**Woven St** (multiple of 20 sts + 2 edge sts)
**Rows 1, 5 and 9 (RS):** K1, *[k2, p2] twice, k12; rep from * to last st, k1.
**Row 2 (and all WS rows):** P1, work all sts as they present themselves to last st, p1.

**Rows 3 and 7:** K1, *k2, [p2, k2] twice, p10; rep from * to last st, k1.
**Rows 11, 15 and 19:** K1, *k12, [p2, k2] twice; rep from * to last st, k1.
**Rows 13 and 17:** K1, *p10, k2, [p2, k2] twice; rep from * to last st, k1.
**Row 20:** Rep Row 2.
Rep Rows 1–20 for pat.

## Pattern Notes
Jacket is worked from shoulders beg with back yoke, followed by front yokes, after which the body is joined and worked to bottom edge; sleeves are worked down from armholes.

Pat is worked back and forth; a circular needle is used to accommodate the large number of sts.

Work all edge sts in St st.

When inc at neck edge, work as follows: At beg of row: k1, M1, continue in pat; at end of row, work in pat to last st, M1, k1.

Neck shaping continues after fronts and back are joined.

Use waste yarn in CC to mark buttonhole positions.

## Instructions
### Back Yoke
Using provisional method and larger needle, cast on 82 (92, 92, 102, 102) sts.

**Row 1 (RS):** Knit.

**Row 2:** Purl.

Beg and end where indicated on Chart A, work in Woven St pat for 9 (9, 10, 10, 10) inches, ending with a WS row.

Place sts on holder.

## Front Yoke
Unzip crochet chain of provisional cast on for first 27 (31, 31, 34, 34) back sts and sl sts to larger needle; unzip next 28 (30, 30, 34, 34) sts and put on holder for back neck; unzip rem 27 (31, 31, 34, 34) back sts and sl to same larger needle.

With RS facing and working both fronts at once with separate balls of yarn, work first st in St st, then beg and end where indicated on Charts B and C, work in Woven St pat to last st, work last st in St st.

## Body
### Shape neck
Inc 1 st at neck edge [every 4th row] 14 times, then [every other row] 1 (2, 2, 4, 4) times, working all new sts in pat as established.

*At the same time*, when fronts measure same as back (ending with the same WS row as on back), cut yarns.

**Joining row (RS):** Attach yarn to neck edge of left front, work in pat as established across left front, cast on 8 (8, 18, 18, 28) sts

continued on 167

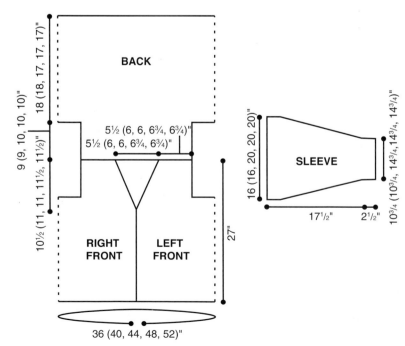

BACK

5½ (6, 6, 6¾, 6¾)"
5½ (6, 6, 6¾, 6¾)"

18 (18, 17, 17, 17)"

9 (9, 10, 10, 10)"

10½ (11, 11, 11½, 11½)"

RIGHT FRONT

LEFT FRONT

27"

36 (40, 44, 48, 52)"

SLEEVE

16 (16, 20, 20, 20)"

10¾ (10¾, 14¾, 14¾, 14¾)"

17½"

2½"

10¾ (10¾, 14¾, 14¾, 14¾)"

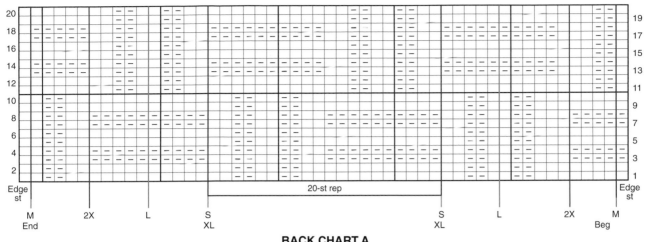

**BACK CHART A**

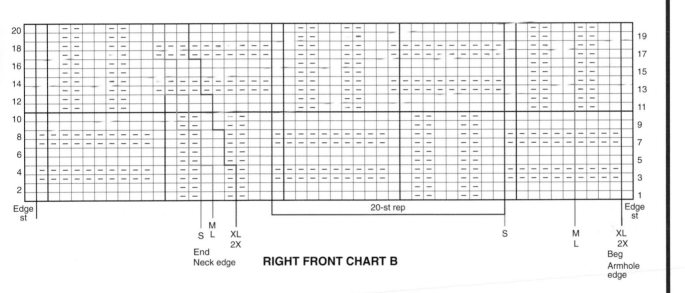

**RIGHT FRONT CHART B**

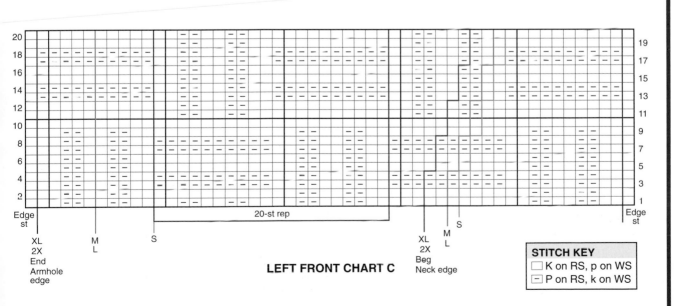

**LEFT FRONT CHART C**

**STITCH KEY**
☐ K on RS, p on WS
⊟ P on RS, k on WS

# sweaters for friends, family & pets

Look here for designs

for best friends,

daughters, sons,

grandchildren, the

men in your life and

pampered pooches.

# school days cardi

Design by Susan Robicheau

Send her off to school wearing a sweater that says you love her! Start at the top with a lacy yoke.

## Skill Level

⬛⬛⬛⬜ INTERMEDIATE

## Sizes

Child's 6 (8, 10, 12, 14) Instructions are given for smallest size, with larger sizes in parentheses. When only 1 number is given, it applies to all sizes.

## Finished Measurements

**Chest:** 25½ (27½, 30½, 32½, 34½) inches (buttoned)
**Length:** 11¾ (12¾, 15½, 17, 19) inches

## Materials

- ▼ Caron Simply Soft Heather 100 percent acrylic medium weight yarn (250 yds/5 oz per skein): 2 (2, 3, 3, 4) skeins autumn heather #9501
- ▼ Size 7 (4.5mm) double-pointed and 29-inch circular needles or size needed to obtain gauge
- ▼ Size J/9 (5.5mm) crochet hook
- ▼ Stitch markers
- ▼ Stitch holder
- ▼ Waste yarn
- ▼ 4 (4, 5, 5, 5) (½-inch) buttons
- ▼ Tapestry needle

## Gauge

16 sts and 24 rows = 4 inches/10cm in St st
To save time, take time to check gauge.

## Special Techniques

**Provisional Cast On:** With crochet hook and waste yarn, make a chain several sts longer than desired cast on. With knitting needle and project yarn, pick up indicated number of sts in the "bumps" on back of chain. When indicated in pat, "unzip" the crochet chain and place live sts on needle or holder.
**Buttonhole:** Work as follows: Yo, k2tog.

## Pattern Stitches

**A. Chevron Panel** (16-st panel)
**Row 1 (WS):** K1, p14, k1.
**Row 2 (RS):** P1, k3, k2tog, yo, k4, yo, ssk, k3, p1.
**Row 3:** K1, p14, k1.
**Row 4:** P1, k2, k2tog, yo, k6, yo, ssk, k2, p1.
**Row 5:** K1, p14, k1.
**Row 6:** P1, k1, k2tog, yo, k2, p4, k2, yo, ssk, k1, p1.
**Row 7:** K1, p5, k4, p5, k1.
**Row 8:** P1, k2tog, yo, k3, p4, k3, yo, ssk, p1.
Rep Rows 1–8 for pat.
**B. Eyelet Welt** (multiple of 2 sts + 2)
**Row 1 (RS):** Purl.
**Row 2:** Knit.

**Row 3:** K1, *k1, sl 1 wyib; rep from * to last st, k1.
**Row 4:** K1, *sl 1 wyif, k1, rep from * to last st, k1.
**Row 5:** K1, *yo, k2tog, rep from * to last st, k1.
**Row 6:** Purl.
Rep Rows 1–6 for pat.

**Pattern Notes**
The sweater begins at the top back yoke which is worked back and forth to the underarm; shoulder sts are picked up for the front yokes and worked to underarm, after which the body is joined and worked to bottom edge. The sleeves are worked in the rnd from the underarm.

The back and front yokes, and lower body are all worked back and forth in rows; a circular needle is used to accommodate the large number of sts.

Charts for the pat sts are included for those preferring to work from charts.

**Back Yoke**
Using provisional method, cast on 50 (54, 60, 64, 68) sts.

**Set-up row (WS):** P1 (2, 3, 3, 4), place marker, work Row 1 of Chevron Panel over next 16 sts, place marker, p16 (18, 22, 26, 28), place marker, work Chevron Panel over next 16 sts, place marker, p1 (2, 3, 3, 4).

Working St st at sides and between the Chevron Panels, continue in pats as

established until 4 (4, 4, 4, 5) reps of Chevron Panel are completed, then work 0 (0, 2, 4, 0) more rows of panel, ending with a RS row.

Sl sts to waste yarn or holder.

**Front Yokes**
Unzip crochet chain of Provisional Cast On for first 17 (19, 21, 22, 23) back sts and sl sts to needle; unzip next 16 (16, 18, 20, 22) sts and sl to waste yarn or holder for back neck; unzip rem 17 (19, 21, 22, 23) back sts and sl to same needle.

Attach yarn to WS of piece and work both fronts at once with separate balls of yarn.

**Set-up row (WS):** Left front: p1 (2, 3, 4, 4), place marker, work Chevron Panel over next 16 sts, place marker, p0 (1, 2, 3, 3); right front: p0 (1, 2, 3, 3), place marker, work Chevron Panel over next 16 sts, place marker, p1 (2, 3, 3, 4).

Working St st on either side of Chevron Panels, work even for 7 more rows, then cable cast on 8 (8, 9, 10, 11) sts at neck edge of each front. (25, 27, 30, 32, 34 sts each front)

Working the cast-on sts in St st, work even until fronts measure same as back, ending on same Chevron pat row.

**Body**
**Sizes 6, 8, 14 only**
**Next row (WS):** Removing markers, purl

across right front, sl back sts from holder to LH needle and purl across, purl across right front. (100, 108, 136 sts)

### Sizes 10, 12 only
**Next row (WS):** Work in pat as established across left front, sl back sts from holder to LH needle and work in pat across. (120, 128 sts)

Continue working in pat for 5 (3) rows, finishing 5th Chevron Panel rep, removing markers on last row.

### All sizes
**Next row (RS):** Knit.

**Next row (WS):** Purl, inc 30 (32, 30, 32, 34) sts evenly spaced across. (130, 140, 150, 160, 170 sts)

Rep [Rows 1–6 of Eyelet Welt] 6 (7, 9, 10, 12) times, then work Rows 1 and 2.

Bind off very loosely.

### Sleeves
With RS facing and using dpns, pick up and knit 40 (40, 44, 48, 52) sts around armhole, place marker for beg of rnd and join.

Purl 2 rnds.

Knit 5 rnds.

**Dec rnd:** K1, k2tog, knit to last 3 sts, ssk, k1. (38, 38, 42, 46, 50 sts)

Continue in St st and rep Dec rnd [every 6th rnd] 8 (9, 10, 11, 12) times. (20, 20, 20, 22, 24 sts)

Work even until sleeve measures approx 9¾ (10¾, 11¾, 12¾, 14) inches or ½ inch less than desired length from armhole.

Purl 4 rnds.

Bind off very loosely.

### Finishing
**Neckband**
With RS facing, pick up and knit 8 (8, 9, 10, 11) sts along right front neck, 4 sts along neck edge, knit 16 (16, 18, 20, 22) back neck sts from holder, pick up and knit 4 sts along

**continued on 168**

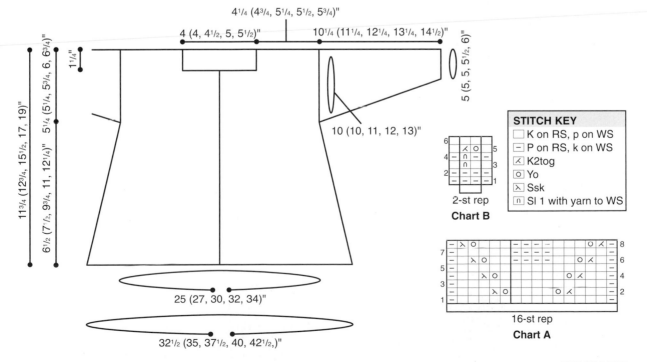

**STITCH KEY**

| | |
|---|---|
| ☐ | K on RS, p on WS |
| − | P on RS, k on WS |
| ⋌ | K2tog |
| ○ | Yo |
| ⋋ | Ssk |
| n | Sl 1 with yarn to WS |

**Chart B**

2-st rep

16-st rep

**Chart A**

4¼ (4¾, 5¼, 5½, 5¾)"

4 (4, 4½, 5, 5½)"

10¼ (11¼, 12¼, 13¼, 14½)"

1¼"

5 (5, 5, 5½, 6)"

11¾ (12¾, 15½, 17, 19)"

5¼ (5¼, 5¾, 6, 6¾)"

6½ (7½, 9¾, 11, 12¼)"

10 (10, 11, 12, 13)"

25 (27, 30, 32, 34)"

32½ (35, 37½, 40, 42½,)"

# shades for play

Design by Sara Louise Harper

Color progression stripes, a rolled-edge trim and an easy raglan increase technique make this pullover quick as well as easy!

## Skill Level
◼◼◻◻ EASY

## Sizes
Child's 4 (6, 8, 10, 12) Instructions are given for smallest size, with larger sizes in parentheses. When only 1 number is given, it applies to all sizes.

## Finished Measurements
**Chest:** 28 (30, 32, 34, 36) inches
**Length:** 14¾ (16, 17¼, 17¾, 19) inches, excluding collar

## Materials
▼ Plymouth Galway Worsted 100 percent wool medium weight yarn (210 yds/100g per ball): 1 (1, 1, 2, 2) balls each light teal #111 (A), light blue #139 (B), and medium blue #116 (C)
▼ Size 8 (5mm) double-pointed and 29-inch circular needles or size needed to obtain gauge
▼ Waste yarn
▼ Stitch markers
▼ Tapestry needle

## Gauge
16 sts and 24 rows = 4 inches/10cm in St st
To save time, take time to check gauge.

## Special Abbreviations
**M1L (Make 1 Left):** Insert LH needle from front to back under the running thread between the last st worked and next st on LH needle. With RH needle, knit into the back of the resulting lp.
**M1R (Make 1 Right):** Insert LH needle from back to front under running thread between the last st worked and next st on LH needle. With RH needle, knit into the front of the resulting lp.
**Pm:** Place marker.

## Pattern Stitch
### Color Progression
*Knit 1 rnd with new color, then 1 rnd with old color; rep from * once, then continue with new color.

## Pattern Notes
This raglan sweater is worked down from the rolled collar. When the yoke is complete, sleeve sts are placed on waste yarn while the

body is completed; sleeves are worked in the rnd from the armhole down.

When measuring the final length, allow edge to roll slightly as it will when worn. The M1 raglan sts are both worked in the same running thread; the 2nd will be tight to work.

### Rolled Collar
With circular needle and A, cast on 72 (74, 76, 78, 78) sts, pm and join, being careful not to twist sts.

Work in St st for 2 inches. Pm in the fabric on last rnd.

### Yoke
**Set-up rnd:** Knit around, placing markers as follows: 22 (24, 26, 28, 30) front sts, pm; 14 (13, 12, 11, 9) sleeve sts, pm, 22 (24, 26, 28, 30) back sts, pm; 14 (13, 12, 11, 9) sleeve sts.

**Raglan Inc rnd:** *Knit to marker, M1L, sl marker, M1R; rep from * to beg of rnd marker, making last M1R following that marker.

Rep Raglan Inc rnd [every other rnd] 16 (17, 18, 19, 20) times. (208, 218, 228, 238, 246 sts)

*At the same time,* when 25 (27, 29, 31, 33) rnds have been worked from the marker, change to B and beg working the Color Progression pat.

### Separate Body & Sleeves
When raglan incs are complete, place 48 (49, 50, 51, 51) sleeve sts on waste yarn.

### Body
Continue working 112 (120, 128, 136, 144)

body sts in St st and *at the same time,* when 25 (27, 29, 31, 33) rnds of B are complete, change to C and work Color Progression pat again.

Continue in C until body measures 9 (10, 11, 11, 12) inches or desired length from underarm.

Bind off all sts very loosely, allowing lower edge to roll.

### Sleeves
Sl sleeve sts to dpns, then pick up and knit 2 sts from underarm, placing beg of rnd marker between them. (50, 51, 52, 53, 53 sts)

Work 3 (3, 4, 4, 6) rnds even in St st.

**Dec rnd:** K1, ssk, knit to last 3 sts, k2tog, k1. (48, 49, 50, 51, 51 sts)

Continue in St st and rep Dec rnd [every 4th (4th, 5th, 5th, 7th) rnd] 11 (11, 11, 11, 10) times. (26, 27, 28, 29, 31 sts)

*At the same time*, when 25 (27, 29, 31, 33) rnds of B are complete, change to C and work Color Progression pat again.

Work even until sleeve measures 8 (9, 10, 11, 12) inches or desired length.

Bind off very loosely, allowing cuff to roll.

**Finishing**
Weave in loose ends. Block to finished measurements. ▼

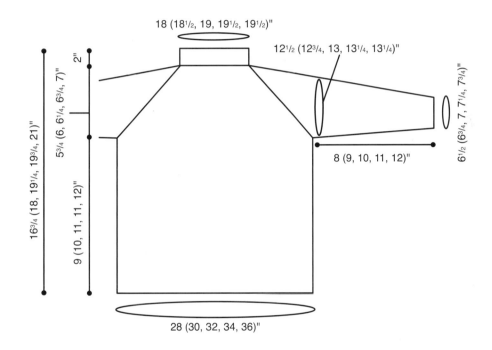

18 (18½, 19, 19½, 19½)"

12½ (12¾, 13, 13¼, 13¼)"

2"

5¾ (6, 6¼, 6¾, 7)"

16¾ (18, 19¼, 19¾, 21)"

9 (10, 11, 11, 12)"

6½ (6¾, 7, 7¼, 7¾)"

8 (9, 10, 11, 12)"

28 (30, 32, 34, 36)"

# ruby layer

**Design by Sara Louise Harper**

Incorporate eyelet detailing while shaping this top-down pullover. It will be a girl's favorite!

## Skill Level
 INTERMEDIATE

## Sizes
Child's 4 (6, 8, 10, 12) Instructions are given for smallest size, with larger sizes in parentheses. When only 1 number is given, it applies to all sizes.

## Finished Measurements
**Chest:** 25¾ (27½, 29¼, 31, 33) inches
**Length:** 14 (15, 16, 16, 17) inches

## Materials
▼ Moda Dea Washable Wool 100 percent superwash merino wool medium weight yarn (166 yds/100g per ball): 2 (3, 3, 3, 4) balls raspberry #4474
▼ Size 8 (5mm) double-pointed and 24-inch circular needles or size needed to obtain gauge
▼ Stitch holders
▼ Stitch markers, 1 in CC for beg of rnd
▼ Tapestry needle

## Gauge
18 sts and 24 rows = 4 inches/10cm in St st
To save time, take time to check gauge.

## Special Abbreviations
**Pm:** Place marker.
**Sm:** Slip marker.

## Pattern Notes
This raglan sweater is worked down from the neck. When the yoke is complete, sleeve sts are placed on waste yarn while the body is completed; sleeves are worked in the rnd from the armhole down.

Midway down the yoke, the sleeves are worked even; however, dec are made to compensate for the yarn over eyelet which continues as a design detail.

## Yoke & Front Neck
With circular needle, cast on 70 (82, 94, 106, 118) sts, placing markers as follows: 1 front st, pm, 2 raglan seam sts, pm, 20 (24, 28, 32, 36) sleeve sts, pm, 2 raglan seam sts, pm, 20 (24, 28, 32, 36) back sts, pm, 2 raglan seam sts, pm, 20 (24, 28, 32, 36) sleeve sts, 2 raglan seam sts, pm, 1 front st; do not join.

## Shape Raglan
**Row 1 (RS):** Yo, k1, yo, sm, *k2, sm, yo, knit to marker, yo, sm; rep from * twice more, k2,

sm, yo, k1. (79, 91, 103, 115, 127 sts)

**Row 2:** Yo, purl to end. (80, 92, 104, 116, 128 sts)

**Row 3:** Yo, knit to marker, yo, sm, *k2, sm, yo, knit to marker, yo, sm; rep from * twice, k2, sm, yo, knit to end of row. (89, 101, 113, 125, 137 sts)

**Row 4:** Rep Row 2. (90, 102, 114, 126, 138 sts)

Continue in this manner [inc 10 sts over 2 rows] 3 more times, ending with a WS row. (120, 132, 144, 156, 168 sts)

**Rnd 1 (RS):** *Knit to marker, yo, sm, k2, sm, yo; rep from * 3 times, knit to end, then cable cast on 8 (12, 16, 20, 24) sts; pm for beg of rnd and join. (136, 152, 168, 184, 200 sts)

Work 1 rnd even, then work raglan inc as established [every other rnd] twice more, ending with a non-inc rnd. (152, 168, 184, 200, 216 sts)

**Next rnd (inc front and back only):** *Knit to marker, yo [right front], sm, k2, sm, yo, k1, ssk, knit to 3 sts before next marker, k2tog, k1, yo, [right sleeve], sm, k2, sm, yo; rep from * once [back and left sleeve], then knit to end of rnd [left and center front]. (156, 172, 188, 204, 220 sts)

Continuing to work yo's before and after raglan seam sts, work sleeves even and inc on front and back [every other rnd] 9 more times, ending on a non-inc rnd. (192, 208, 224, 240, 256 sts)

**Separate Sleeves From Body**
**Next rnd:** Removing markers, knit to marker, then k1 raglan st; sl next 38 (42, 46, 50, 54) sts to waste yarn for sleeve; k1 raglan seam st, knit across back sts, k1 raglan seam st; sl next 38 (42, 46, 50, 54) sts to waste yarn for sleeve; pm for new beg of rnd and join. (116, 124, 132, 140, 148 sts)

**Body**
Work in St st for 4½ (5½, 6½, 6½, 7½) inches.

**Eyelet rnd:** *Yo, k2tog; rep from * around.

*Knit 4 rnds, work 1 Eyelet rnd; rep from * once, then knit 3 rnds.

Work 4 rnds in K1, P1 rib.

Bind off very loosely in rib.

## Sleeves

Sl sts from waste yarn to dpns.

Knit 6 rnds.

Work Eyelet rnd.

Knit 1 rnd.

Work 3 rnds in K1, P1 rib.

Bind off loosely in rib.

## Finishing

### Neckband

With circular needle, pick up and knit 102 (112, 124, 136, 146) sts evenly around neck, pm for beg of rnd and join.

Work 4 rnds in K1, P1 rib.

Bind off all sts firmly in ribbing.

Weave in loose ends. Block to finished measurements. ▼

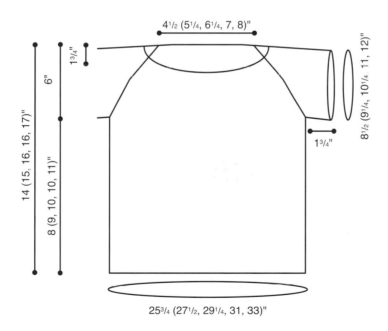

# styled for fun

Design by Susan Robicheau

Use a comfortable yarn and start at the top.
All the kids will love this unisex style.

## Skill Level

◼◼◻◻ EASY

## Sizes

Child's 6 (8, 10, 12, 14) Instructions are given for smallest size, with larger sizes in parentheses. When only 1 number is given, it applies to all sizes.

## Finished Measurements

**Chest:** 26½ (28¾, 31¼, 33½, 36) inches
**Length:** 12¼ (14½, 16¼, 18, 18) inches

## Materials

- ▼ Berroco Comfort 50 percent super-fine nylon/50 percent super-fine acrylic medium weight yarn (210 yds/100g per ball): 2 (3, 5, 6, 8) balls olive #9781
- ▼ Size 5 (3.75mm) double-pointed, 16- and 24-inch circular needles
- ▼ Size 7 (4.5mm) double-pointed and 24-inch circular needles or size needed to obtain gauge
- ▼ Size J/9 (5.5mm) crochet hook
- ▼ Waste yarn
- ▼ Stitch holders
- ▼ Tapestry needle

## Gauge

20 sts and 28 rows = 4 inches/10cm in pat st with larger needle
To save time, take time to check gauge.

## Special Technique

**Provisional Cast On:** With crochet hook and waste yarn, make a chain several sts longer than desired cast on. With knitting needle and project yarn, pick up indicated number of sts in the "bumps" on back of chain. When indicated in pat, "unzip" the crochet chain and place live sts on needle or holder.

## Pattern Stitch

**Woven St** (multiple of 6 sts)
**Rows/Rnds 1 (RS)–3:** *K3, p3; rep from * to end.
**Rows/Rnds 4–6:** Work in rev St st.
**Rows/Rnds 7–9:** Rep Row 1.
**Rows/Rnds 10–12:** Work in St st.
Rep Rows 1–12 for pat.

## Pattern Notes

The sweater is worked from the shoulders down to underarm; body is joined and worked in the rnd to bottom; sleeves are worked in the rnd from armhole.

A chart for the Woven St pat is included for those preferring to work from charts; when working pat in the round, read all chart rows from right to left.

### Back Yoke

Using provisional method and larger needle, cast on 66 (72, 78, 84, 90) sts; do not join.

Work in Woven St pat for approx 5¼ (5½, 6, 6½, 7¼) inches.

Cut yarn and sl sts to waste yarn or holder.

### Front Yoke & Neck

Unzip crochet chain of provisional cast on for first 21 (24, 24, 27, 30) back sts and sl sts to larger needle; unzip next 24 (24, 30, 30, 30) sts and sl to waste yarn or holder for back neck; unzip rem 21 (24, 24, 27, 30) back sts and sl to same larger needle.

Work both sides of neck at once with separate balls of yarn.

**Set-up row (RS):** Right front: *K3, p3; rep from * to last 3 (0, 0, 3, 0) sts, k3; left front: p3 (0, 0, 3, 0), *k3, p3; rep from * to end.

Continue in Woven St pat as established for 7 (9, 5, 5, 9) rows.

Inc at each neck edge on next, then [every other row] 2 (3, 5, 5, 5) times, ending with a WS row. (24, 28, 30, 33, 36 sts each side)

Cut yarn on left front.

**Next row (RS):** Work across right front, cast on 18 (16, 18, 18) front neck sts, work across left front.

Work even in pat as established, until front measures same as back, ending on same pat row as for back.

### Body

**Rnd 1:** Work in pat across front, sl back sts from holder to LH needle and work in pat across, place marker for beg of rnd and join. (132, 144, 156, 168, 180 sts)

Work even in pat as established until body measures approx 5 (6½, 7¾, 9, 8¼) inches or 2 (2½, 2½, 2½, 2½) inches short of desired length from underarm.

Change to smaller needle and work in K1, P1 Rib for 2 (2½, 2½, 2½, 2½) inches.

Bind off very loosely in rib.

### Sleeves

Using larger dpns and beg at underarm, pick up and knit 48 (54, 60, 66, 72) sts around armhole, place marker for beg of rnd and join.

Working in Woven St pat, work 2 rnds even.

**Next rnd:** K1, k2tog, work in pat to last 3 sts, p2tog, p1. (46, 52, 58, 64, 70 sts)

Continue in pat and dec in pat at beg and end of rnd [every 6th rnd] 10 (12, 13, 15, 15) times. (26, 28, 32, 34, 40 sts)

Work even until sleeve measures approx 10¼ (12, 12, 13¾, 13¾) inches or 1 (1, 1½, 1½, 2¼) inches short of desired length.

Change to smaller dpns and work K1, P1 Rib for 1 (1, 1½, 1½, 2¼) inches.

Bind off very loosely in rib.

### Neckband

With RS facing and using smaller dpns, knit 24 (24, 30, 30, 30) back sts from holder, pick up and knit 13 (15, 15, 15, 17) sts along left side of neck, 18 (16, 18, 18, 18) front neck sts, and 13 (15, 15, 15, 17) sts along right side of neck. (68, 70, 78, 78, 82 sts)

Work in K1, P1 Rib for 1 inch.

Bind off very loosely in rib. Weave in all ends. Block to finished measurements. ▼

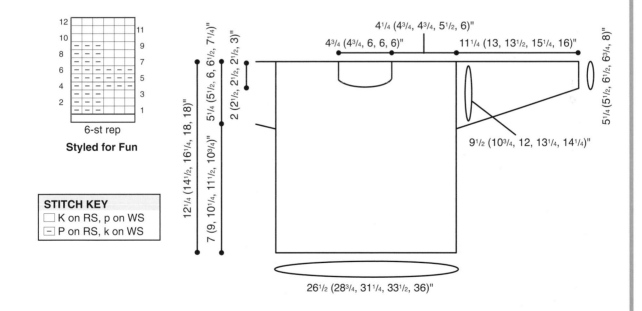

12

10

8

6

4

2

11

9

7

5

3

1

6-st rep

**Styled for Fun**

**STITCH KEY**
☐ K on RS, p on WS
⊟ P on RS, k on WS

12¼ (14½, 16¼, 18, 18)"

7 (9, 10¼, 11½, 10¾)"

5¼ (5½, 6, 6½, 7¼)"

2 (2½, 2½, 2½, 3)"

4¼ (4¾, 4¾, 5½, 6)"

4¾ (4¾, 6, 6, 6)"

11¼ (13, 13½, 15¼, 16)"

5¼ (5½, 6½, 6¾, 8)"

9½ (10¾, 12, 13¼, 14¼)"

26½ (28¾, 31¼, 33½, 36)"

# give him a vee

**Design by Joyce Nordstrom**

You can't beat the classic good looks of this V-neck sweater. It can be tried on to test the fit as it is knit.

## Skill Level

 INTERMEDIATE

## Sizes

Man's small (medium, large, extra large)
Instructions are given for smallest size, with larger sizes in parentheses. When only 1 number is given, it applies to all sizes.

## Finished Measurements

**Chest:** 40½ (44½, 48½, 52½) inches
**Length:** 25¾ (28¼, 30¼, 31¾) inches

## Materials

▼ Moda Dea Vision 65 percent wool/35 percent acrylic medium weight yarn (155 yds/100g per ball): 6 (7, 8, 9) balls glade #2955
▼ Size 7 (4.5mm) double-pointed needles
▼ Size 9 (5.5mm) double-point, 16- and 29-inch circular needles or size needed to obtain gauge.
▼ Stitch markers, 1 in CC for beg of rnd
▼ Waste yarn
▼ Tapestry needle

## Gauge

16 sts and 22 rows = 4 inches/10cm in Faux Rib with larger needles
To save time, take time to check gauge.

## Special Abbreviations

**Pm:** Place marker.
**Sm:** Slip marker.

## Pattern Stitch

**Faux Rib** (multiple of 8 sts)
**Row 1 (RS):** K7, sl 1 purlwise.
**Row 2:** Purl.
Work Rows 1 and 2 for pat.
*Note: When working in the rnd, knit Rnd 2.*

## Pattern Notes

This raglan pullover is worked down from top yoke. When yoke is complete, the body and sleeves are separated. The sleeves and body are worked separately in the rnd from the underarm.

Work raglan seam sts in St st.

On sleeves, change to dpns when sts no longer fit comfortably on circular needle.

## Yoke

With larger 29-inch needle, loosely cast on 55 (55, 55, 63) sts. Do not join.

**Row 1 (WS):** Purl across, placing markers as follows: 1 (1, 1, 2) front st(s), pm, 1 raglan seam st, pm, 11 (11, 11, 13) sleeve sts, pm, 1 raglan seam st, pm, 27 (27, 27 29) back sts, pm, 1 raglan seam st, pm, 11 (11, 11, 13) sleeve sts, pm, 1 raglan seam st, pm, 1 (1, 1, 2) front st(s).

### Beg Raglan & V-Neck Shaping

**Set-up row:** K1 (1, 1, 2), M1; sm, k1, sm; M1, k1 (1, 1, 2), sl 1, k7, sl 1, k1 (1, 1, 2), M1; sm, k1, sm; M1, k1 (1, 1, 2), sl 1, [k7, sl 1] 3 times, k1 (1, 1, 2), M1; sm, k1, sm; M1, [k1 (1, 1, 2), sl 1, k7, sl 1, k1, (1, 1, 2), M1; sm, k1, sm; M1, k 1 (1, 1, 2). (63, 63, 63, 71 sts)

**Row 2:** Purl.

Continue inc on both sides of raglan seam sts [every other row] 26 (30, 34, 37) times, working new sts into Faux Rib pat as they accumulate, and *at the same time,* inc 1 st at each neck edge [every 4th row] 12 (9, 6, 3) times, then [every 5th row] 1 (4, 7, 10) times, working last neck inc on 1 front only for correct pat placement, and ending on a RS row.

### Join Fronts

With RS still facing, join by working across left front sts; exchange next marker for beg of rnd marker in CC.

Continue in pat as established around and complete raglan inc, ending with Rnd 2 of pat. (296, 328, 360, 392 sts)

Sl front and back and right sleeve sts to separate pieces of waste yarn, including raglan seam sts with front or back sts. (83, 91, 99, 107 front/back sts; 65, 73, 81, 89 sleeve sts)

## Sleeves

Change to 16-inch circular needle and continue on left sleeve sts only; pm for beg of rnd at center underarm and join.

Work 6 rnds even in pat as established.

**Dec rnd:** Ssk, work in pat to last 2 sts, k2tog. (63, 71, 79, 87 sts)

Rep Dec rnd [every 6th rnd] 9 (9, 7, 9) times, then [every 4th rnd] 5 (6, 10, 8) times. (35, 41, 45, 53 sts)

Work even until sleeve measures 15½ (16, 17, 17½) inches from underarm, or 2½ inches short of desired length.

Change to smaller dpns and work in K1, P1 rib, dec 1 st on first rnd. (34, 40, 44, 52 sts)

Work even for 2½ inches.

Bind off very loosely in ribbing.

Rep for right sleeve.

## Body

Sl front and back sts from waste yarn to larger circular needle.

**Rnd 1:** *K2tog, work in pat to last 2 sts of back, k2tog; rep from * across front, pm for beg of rnd and join. (162, 178, 194, 210 sts)

Work in pat as established until body measures 13½, (14½, 15, 15½) inches from underarm or 2½ inches short of desired length.

Changing to smaller needles, work even in K1, P1 rib for 2½ inches.

Bind off all sts very loosely.

## Finishing

### Neckband

With RS facing and using smaller 16-inch circular needle, beg at back shoulder seam,

pick up and knit 55 (55, 55, 63) sts around back of neck, 48 (54, 60, 68) sts along front neck to bottom of V, place marker, 1 st in point, pm, 48, (54, 60, 68) sts along front neck to beg of rnd; place marker for beg of rnd and join. (152, 164, 176, 200 sts)

**Set-up rnd:** P1, *k1, p1; rep from * to 2 sts before first marker, ssk, sl marker, k1, sl marker, k2tog, *p1, k1; rep from * to end of rnd.

Continue in rib as established and dec in pat on either side of V [every rnd] until neckband measures 1¼ inches.

Bind off in rib.

Weave in all ends. Block to finished measurements. ▼

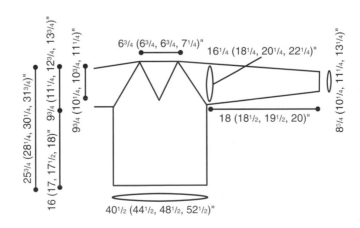

# rugged ribbed sweater

Design by Pauline Schultz

This stretchy style will move easily with the action. It's a great way to give your guy a ribbing!

## Skill Level
■■■□ EXPERIENCED

## Sizes
Man's small (medium, large, extra-large, 2X-large, 3X-large) Instructions are given for smallest size, with larger sizes in parentheses. When only 1 number is given, it applies to all sizes.

## Finished Measurements
**Chest:** 40 (44, 48, 52, 58, 62) inches
**Length:** 27 (28½, 29, 29½, 30, 30½) inches, excluding collar

## Materials
▼ Bernat Denimstyle 70 percent acrylic/30 percent cotton medium weight yarn (196 yds/100g per ball): 6 (6, 7, 8, 8, 9) balls indigo #03108
▼ Size 6 (4mm) double-point and 29-inch circular needles
▼ Size 8 (5mm) double-pointed, 16- and 29-inch circular needles or size needed to obtain gauge
▼ Stitch markers, 1 in CC for beg of rnd
▼ Stitch holders
▼ Waste yarn
▼ Tapestry needle

## Gauge
20 sts and 28 rows = 5 inches/12.5cm in Cable Rib with larger needle
To save time, take time to check gauge.

## Special Abbreviations
**RT (Right Twist):** K2tog, leaving sts on LH needle; insert RH needle from the front between the 2 sts just knitted tog, and knit the first st again; sl both sts from the needle tog.
**Dec1 (Decrease 1):** K2tog (or p2tog) as necessary to maintain rib pat.
**Inc1 (Increase 1):** Knit (or purl) in front and back of next st as necessary to maintain pat.

## Special Technique
**Provisional Cast On:** With crochet hook and waste yarn, make a chain several sts longer than desired cast on. With knitting needle and project yarn, pick up indicated number of sts in the "bumps" on back of chain. When indicated in pat, "unzip" the crochet chain to free live sts.

## Pattern Stitch
**Cabled Rib** (multiple of 4 sts + 2)
**Row 1 (RS):** *P2, k2; rep from * to last 2 sts, p2.
**Row 2:** *K2, p2; rep from * to last 2 sts, k2.

**Row 3:** *P2, RT; rep from * to last 2 sts, p2.
**Row 4:** Rep Row 2.
Rep Rows 1–4 for pat.
When working in rnds, continue in rib as established.

**Pattern Notes**
Read through instructions carefully before beginning; shaping on sleeves and body occurs simultaneously.

Sweater begins with saddle-shoulder yoke, which is worked in 2 parts from the center out; back and front sts are picked up from edges of saddle-shoulder yoke and worked down for several rows each, after which sleeve sts, worked from outer sides of shoulder yoke, are incorporated and all pieces are worked *at the same time* to underarm. At that point, the sleeves are worked down to cuff, then the body is worked down to bottom edge.

Sections in upper yoke are worked back and forth on a circular needle until the front neck is joined, after which lower yoke, body and sleeves are worked in the rnd.

For sleeves, change to dpns when sts no longer fit comfortably on circular needle.

Edge sts are worked in St st until they are incorporated into the pat st as indicated in pat.

### Saddle-Shoulder Yoke & Back Neck
**First side**
Using provisional method and larger needle, cast on 14 (18, 18, 22, 22, 22) sts.

Work in Cabled Rib pat for 2¾ (2¾, 3, 3, 3¼, 3¼) inches, ending with a WS row.

**Next row (RS):** Cast on 16 (16, 16, 16, 16, 20) sts, then work across all sts maintaining continuity of Cabled Rib pat. (30, 34, 34, 38, 38, 42 sts)

Work even for 5 (5½, 5¾, 5¾, 6, 6½) inches, ending with Row 2 or 4 and noting row number for future reference.

Sl sts to holder.

**Second side**
"Unzip" provisional cast on and sl live sts to larger needle.

Work as for first side of yoke, ending on same row.

Sl sts to holder.

### Back
**Row 1 (RS):** Pick up and knit 70 (74, 80, 84, 90, 94) sts along long straight (back) edge of yoke.

**Row 2 (dec):** P1 (edge st), work across in Cabled Rib beg with Row 2 and work dec in pat as follows: Cabled Rib 4 (3, 3, 3, 3, 5), *Dec1, Cabled Rib 4 (5, 4, 4, 3, 3); rep from * 2

(2, 3, 3, 4, 4) times, Cabled Rib 24 (24, 24, 28, 32, 32), *Cabled Rib 4 (5, 4, 4, 3, 3), Dec1; rep from * 2 (2, 3, 3, 4, 4) times, Cabled Rib to last st, p1 (edge st). (64, 68, 72, 76, 80, 84 sts)

Maintaining edge sts in St st, work 3 pat reps plus 2 extra rows (if necessary) to end on same row as yoke.

Sl sts to waste yarn for holder.

### Right Front
**Row 1 (RS):** Pick up and knit 23 (25, 28, 28, 29, 31) sts along short right front edge of yoke.

**Sizes Small, Large, Extra-Large, 2X-Large only**
**Row 2 (set up pat and dec):** P1, then beg with Row 2 of pat, continue in Cabled Rib to last st and *at the same time,* dec 3 (4, 4, 5) sts in pat evenly spaced across, end p1 (edge st). (20, 24, 24, 24 sts rem)

**Sizes Medium, 3X-Large only**
**Row 2 (set up pat and dec):** K1, p2, then beg with Row 2 of pat, continue in Cabled Rib to last st and *at the same time,* dec 3 (5) sts in pat evenly spaced across, end p1 (edge st). (22, 26 sts rem)

**All Sizes**
Maintaining edge st in St st, work 3 pat reps plus 2 extra rows (if necessary) to end on same row as yoke.

Place sts on holder.

### Left Front
**Row 1 (RS):** Pick up and knit 23 (25, 28, 28, 29, 31) sts along short left front edge of yoke.

**Row 2 (set up pat and dec):** P1 (edge st), then beg with Row 2 of pat, work Cabled Rib pat to end, and *at the same time,* dec 3 (3, 4, 4, 5, 5) sts in pat evenly spaced across. (20, 22, 24, 24, 24, 26 sts)

Maintaining edge st in St st, work 3 pat reps

plus 2 extra rows (if necessary) to end of same row as yoke.

### Join Body & Sleeves
**Row 1 (RS):** Work right front to edge st, place marker for sleeve, knit edge st, then pick up and knit 5 sts along left front edge; work 30 (34, 34, 38, 38, 42) saddle sts from holder; pick up and knit 5 sts along back left edge; knit edge st, place marker for sleeve, work back sts to edge st, place marker for sleeve, knit edge st; pick up and knit 5 sts along back right edge; work saddle sts from holder; pick up and knit 5 sts along right front edge; knit edge st, place marker for sleeve, work right front sts. (42, 46, 46, 50, 50, 54 sts each sleeve; 62, 66, 70, 74, 78, 82 sts on back; 19, 21, 23, 23, 23, 25 sts each front)

**Row 2:** Work in Cable Rib as established, incorporating edge sts and picked-up sts into pat.

**Sleeve Inc Row:** *Work in pat to marker, sl marker, Inc1, work to 1 st before marker, Inc1, sl marker; rep from * to last marker, work in pat to end. (44, 48, 48, 52, 52, 56 sts each sleeve)

Rep Sleeve Inc Row [every 7th (7th, 6th, 8th, 7th, 7th) row/rnd] 6 (6, 8, 6, 8, 8) times, incorporating new sts into pat as established on sleeves. (56, 60, 64, 64, 68, 72 sts each sleeve)

Work even until body armscye shaping below is complete.

### Join Front Neck
*At the same time,* when fronts measure 3¼ (2¾, 3¼, 3¾, 4¼, 3¾) inches from saddle, ending with a WS row, cut yarn, and join front neck as follows: sl right front sts to LH needle and re-attach yarn (this will be beg of rnd, place CC marker); work across right front, cable cast on 24 (24, 24, 28, 32, 32) sts to RH needle for front neck, work around left front, sleeve, back and sleeve to end of rnd.

(62, 66, 70, 74, 78, 82 front sts)

## Shape Body Armscye

Beg with the 6th (6th, 7th, 5th, 6th, 6th) Sleeve Inc Row, Inc1 on front and back sides of markers [every 3rd rnd] 1 (0, 0, 2, 2) time(s), [every other rnd] 1 (3, 3, 3, 3, 3) time(s), and [every rnd] 3 (4, 6, 4, 6 10) times, working new sts in pat as established between markers. (56, 60, 64, 64, 68, 72 sts each sleeve; 72, 80, 88, 92, 104, 112 sts each front and back)

## Separate Sleeves From Body

When all shaping is complete, sl front, back and left sleeve sts to separate lengths of waste yarn; sl right sleeve sts to 16-inch circular needle.

## Right Sleeve

**Rnd 1:** At underarm, cast on 4 (4, 4, 6, 6, 6) sts, work in pat across, cast on 4 (4, 4, 6, 6, 6) sts, place marker for beg of rnd. (64, 68, 72, 76, 80, 84 sts)

Work 2 rnds even in pat as established, working underarm sts into pat.

**Dec Rnd:** Dec1, work in pat to 2 sts before marker, Dec1. (62, 66, 70, 74, 78, 82 sts)

Rep Dec Rnd [every 6th rnd] 15 (15, 16, 16, 17, 17) times. (32, 36, 38, 42, 44, 48 sts)

Work even until sleeve measures 18 (18½, 19, 19, 19½, 19½) inches from underarm or desired length from underarm.

Bind off in rib.

## Left Sleeve

Sl left sleeve sts to 16-inch circular needle and work as for right sleeve.

## Body

Sl front and back sts to larger 29-inch needle.

**Rnd 1:** Work across front; pick up and knit 8 (8, 8, 12, 12, 12) sts from right sleeve underarm; work across back; pick up and knit 8 (8, 8, 12, 12, 12) sts from left sleeve underarm, place marker for beg of rnd. (160, 176, 192, 208, 224, 240 sts)

Work even in pat as established, incorporating picked-up sts into pat, until body measures 15½ (16, 16, 16, 15, 15) inches or desired length from underarm.

Bind off very loosely in rib.

## Collar

With RS facing and using smaller circular

needle, beg at lower right corner, pick up and knit 1 st in each row or st around neck to lower left corner, ending in an uneven number of sts. ***Note:*** *Do not pick up along front neck cast-on edge.*

Work in rib pat as follows:

**Row 1 (WS):** Sl 1, *p1, k1; rep from * to last 2 sts, p2.

**Row 2:** Sl 1, *k1, p1; rep from * to last 2 sts, k2.

Rep Rows 1 and 2 until ribbing reaches comfortably across neck opening without stretching.

### Finishing

Sew collar edges to lower neck opening, left over right.

Weave in all ends. Block to finished measurements. ▼

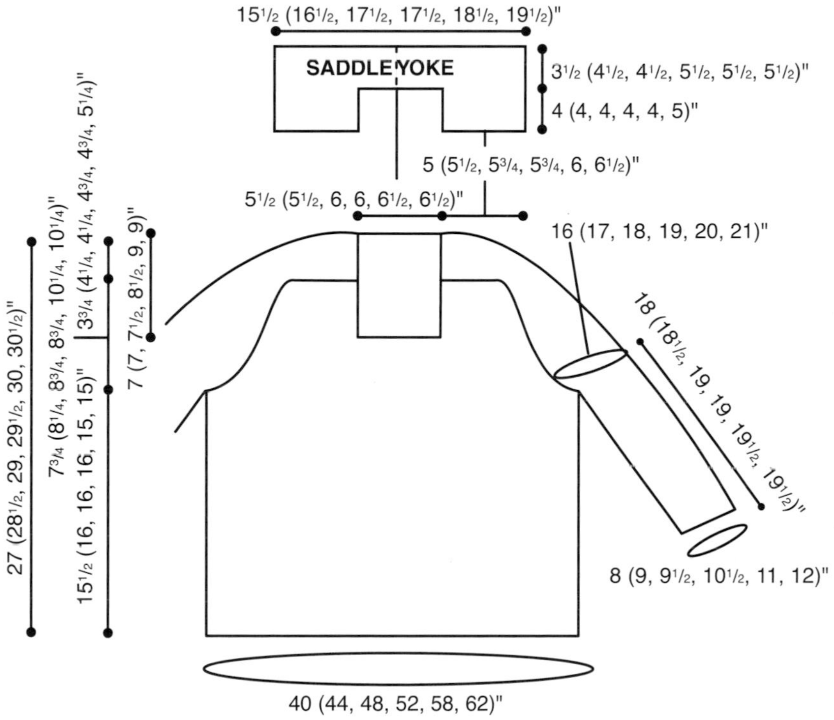

15½ (16½, 17½, 17½, 18½, 19½)"
SADDLE YOKE
3½ (4½, 4½, 5½, 5½, 5½)"
4 (4, 4, 4, 4, 5)"
5 (5½, 5¾, 5¾, 6, 6½)"
5½ (5½, 6, 6, 6½, 6½)"
16 (17, 18, 19, 20, 21)"
18 (18½, 19, 19, 19½, 19½)"
8 (9, 9½, 10½, 11, 12)"
27 (28½, 29, 29½, 30, 30½)"
7¾ (8¼, 8¾, 8¾, 10¼, 10¼)"
15½ (16, 16, 16, 15, 15)"
3¾ (4¼, 4¼, 4¾, 4¾, 5¼)"
7 (7, 7½, 8½, 9, 9)"
40 (44, 48, 52, 58, 62)"

# toasty friend

Design by Cecily Glowik

Choose this soft layer for keeping shoulders warm and cozy. It's a great choice for any age!

## Skill Level
◼◻◻◻ EASY

## Sizes
Woman's small (medium, large, extra-large, 2X-large) Instructions are given for smallest size, with larger sizes in parentheses. When only 1 number is given, it applies to all sizes.

## Finished Measurements
**Bottom circumference:** 48 (51½, 54¾, 58¼, 61¾) inches
**Length to collar:** 13½ (13½, 14½, 14½, 14½) inches

## Materials
▼ Plymouth Baby Alpaca Grande 100 percent baby alpaca bulky weight yarn (110 yds/100g per skein): 5 (5, 6, 6, 7) skeins light brown #202
▼ Size 10½ (6.5mm) 16-, 29- and 36-inch circular needles or size needed to obtain gauge
▼ Size 11 (8mm) 16-inch circular needle (optional)
▼ Stitch markers, 1 in CC for beg of rnd
▼ Tapestry needle

## Gauge
14 sts and 20 rows = 4 inches/10cm in St st
To save time, take time to check gauge.

## Special Abbreviation
**Inc1 (lifted increase):** Inc 1 st as follows: before marker—k1 in row below next st, k1; following marker—k1, k1 2 rows below last st worked.

## Pattern Stitch
**Lace Pattern** (multiple of 12 sts)
**Rnd 1:** *P3, yo, k4, k2tog, k3, rep from * around.
**Rnd 2:** *P3, k1, yo, k4, k2tog, k2, rep from * around.
**Rnd 3:** *P3, k2, yo, k4, k2tog, k1, rep from * around.
**Rnd 4:** *P3, k3, yo, k4, k2tog, rep from * around.
Rep Rnds 1–4 for pat.

## Pattern Notes
Wrap begins with long collar, followed by a raglan-shaped body.

Change to longer needle when sts no longer fit comfortably on needle in use.

A chart for the Lace pat is included for those preferring to work from charts.

(Optional) Cast on and bind off with a needle 1 size larger than project needle to ensure loose edges.

### Wrap
### Collar
With 16-inch needle, loosely cast on 64 (64, 72, 72, 80) sts, place marker for beg of rnd and join, being careful not to twist sts.

Work even in K4, P4 rib for 10 inches.

### Body
**Next rnd:** *K4, M1, p4, M1, rep from * around. (80, 80, 90, 90, 100 sts)

Work 4 rnds in K4, P6 rib.

Work 4 rnds in St st.

**Next rnd:** *K30 (30, 33, 33, 36), place marker, k10 (10, 12, 12, 14), place marker; rep from * once to end of rnd marker.

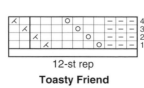

12-st rep

**Toasty Friend**

**Inc rnd:** *Inc1, knit to marker, Inc1, sl marker; rep from * around. (88, 88, 98, 98, 108, 108 sts)

Rep Inc rnd [every other rnd] 2 (4, 4, 5, 5) times, then [every 4th rnd] 8 times. (168, 184, 194, 202, 212 sts)

Work even in St st until piece measures approx 8½ (8½, 9½, 9½, 9½) inches from end of rib or 5 inches less than desired length.

**Next rnd:** Knit, and inc 0 (dec 4, dec 2, inc 2, inc 4) sts evenly around. (168, 180, 192, 204, 216 sts)

[Rep Rnds 1–4 of Lace pat] 5 times, then work Rnds 1–3.

Bind off very loosely in pat using larger needle if necessary.

### Finishing
Weave in ends. Block piece to finished measurements. ▼

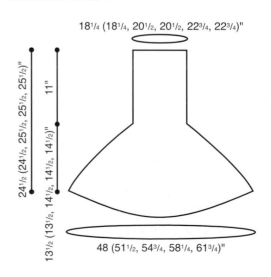

18¼ (18¼, 20½, 20½, 22¾, 22¾)"

24½ (24½, 25½, 25½, 25½)"

11"

13½ (13½, 14½, 14½, 14½)"

48 (51½, 54¾, 58¼, 61¾)"

# down & doggie

Design by Kathy Wesley

Don't forget that the little doggie that is always there for you deserves a stylish top-down sweater too!

## Skill Level
 EASY

## Sizes
Small (medium, large) Instructions are given for smallest size, with larger sizes in parentheses. When only 1 number is given, it applies to all sizes.

## Measurements
**Center length to neck:** 10 (14, 20) inches
**Width (without tabs):** 9 (12½, 17) inches

## Materials
▼ Plymouth/Kaos Series Collection Confusion wool/acrylic blend bulky weight yarn (109 yds/65–75g per skein): 1 (1, 2) skeins green tones #1 (MC)
▼ Plymouth/Bristol Yarn Gallery Yardley 76 percent baby alpaca/19 percent silk/5 percent nylon medium weight yarn (109 yds/50g per ball): 1 ball brown #302 (CC)
▼ Size 10½ (6.5mm) straight needles or size needed to obtain gauge
▼ 2-inch length hook-and-loop fastener
▼ 2 (⅝-inch) gold buttons

### Gauge
14 sts and 24 rows = 4 inches/10cm in garter st
To save time, take time to check gauge.

### Body
Beg at neck edge with CC, cast on 26 (34, 50) sts

Work in St st until piece measures 2 (2, 2½) inches, ending with a WS row.

Change to MC.

**Next row:** Knit, inc 4 (6, 6) sts evenly spaced across. (30, 40, 56 sts)

Continue in garter st and inc 1 st each end [every 8 rows] 1 (2, 2) times. (32, 44, 60 sts)

Work even in garter st until piece measures 6 (10, 16) inches.

**Dec row:** K1, ssk, knit to last 3 sts, k2tog, k1. (30, 42, 58 sts)

Continue in garter st and rep Dec row [every other row] 5 (6, 9) times. (20, 30, 40 sts)

**Next row:** K2 tog across. (10, 15, 20 sts)

Bind off.

### Belly Tab
Make 2
With CC, cast on 10 sts.

Work in garter st for 2 (3, 4) inches.

**Next row:** [K1, k2tog] 3 times, k1. (7 sts)

**Next row:** Knit.

**Next row:** [K1, k2tog] twice, k1. (5 sts)

**Next row:** Knit.

Bind off.

### Finishing
Weave in all ends.

Allow St st collar to roll to outside. Referring to photo, sew buttons to each edge of collar through both thicknesses of collar.

Sew tabs centered 2 (3, 4) inches along each side. Sew hook-and-loop fastener to ends of each tab to close coat under dog's stomach.

### Twisted Cord
With CC, cut 8-foot length. Fold in half twice. Make overhand knots at both ends. Anchor 1 end and twist until cord begins to double back. Knot 2 ends tog and allow twists to form cord. Trim below knot to form tassel. Push button through 1 end. Adjust to fit by placing 2nd button where needed along twisted cord. ▼

# togs for baby & toddler

Here's a selection of fun styles to welcome a new baby and to dress the active toddler.

# natural beauty for baby

Design by Nazanin S. Fard

Welcome Baby to the world with a wonderfully patterned top-down raglan sleeve sweater with matching hat.

## Skill Level
■■□□ EASY

## Sizes
Newborn (6 months, 12 months) Instructions are given for smallest size, with larger sizes in parentheses. When only 1 number is given, it applies to all sizes.

## Finished Measurements
**Chest:** 19¼ (23¼, 25¼) inches
**Length:** 9¾ (11½, 12) inches
**Hat circumference:** 15 inches

## Materials
▼ Bernat Soy 50 percent soy/50 percent acrylic medium weight yarn (134 yds/70g per ball): 3 (3, 4) balls oatmeal #15008
▼ Size 6 (4mm) double-pointed and 29-inch circular needles or size needed to obtain gauge
▼ Size F/5 (3.75 mm) crochet hook
▼ Stitch markers
▼ Tapestry needle
▼ Waste yarn
▼ 4 (⁷⁄₁₆-inch) buttons

## Gauge
20 sts and 28 rows = 4 inches/10cm in St st
To save time, take time to check gauge.

## Special Abbreviations
**Pm:** Place marker.
**Sm:** Slip marker.

## Pattern Stitch
**Lace Pat** (multiple of 5 sts)
**Row/Rnd 1:** *K2tog, k3, yo; rep from * to end.
**Row 2 and all WS rows:** Purl.
***Note:** When working in the rnd, knit all even-numbered rnds.*
**Row/Rnd 3:** *K2tog, k2, yo, k1; rep from * to end.
**Row/Rnd 5:** *K2tog, k1, yo, k2; rep from * to end.
**Row/Rnd 7:** *K2tog, yo, k3; rep from * to end.
**Row/Rnd 9:** *Yo, k3, ssk; rep from * to end.
**Row/Rnd 11:** *K1, yo, k2, ssk; rep from * to end.
**Row/Rnd 13:** *K2, yo, k1, ssk; rep from * to end.
**Row/Rnd 15:** *K3, yo, ssk; rep from * to end.
**Row/Rnd 16:** Purl. (Knit if working in the rnd.)
Rep Rows 1–16 for pat.

## Pattern Notes

This sweater is worked from the raglan yoke down, after which the body is worked. The sleeves are worked in the rnd from the yoke down.

The yokes and lower body are worked back and forth on a circular needle.

A chart for Lace pat is included for those preferring to work from charts.

## Sweater

### Yoke

Cast on 34 (36, 40) sts, do not join.

**Set-up row (RS):** Knit across, placing markers as follows: 1 front st, pm, 1 raglan seam st, pm, 6 (5, 7) sleeve sts, pm, 1 raglan seam st, pm, 16 (20, 20) back sts, pm, 1 raglan seam st, pm, 6 (5, 7) sleeve sts, pm, 1 raglan seam st, pm, 1 front st.

**Row 2 and all WS rows:** Purl.

**Raglan Inc row:** *Knit to marker, M1, sm, k1, sm, M1; rep from *, knit to end. (42, 44, 48 sts sts)

### Shape Front Neck

**Next row (RS):** Knit in front and back of first st, *knit to marker, M1, sm, k1, sm, M1; rep from * , then knit to last st, knit in front and back of last st. (52, 54, 58 sts)

Rep [Row 5] 2 (3, 4) times, ending with a WS row. (72, 84, 98 sts)

**Next row (RS):** Cast on 5 (6, 7) sts, *knit to marker, M1, sm, k1, sm, M1; rep from *, knit to end, then cast on 5 (6, 7) sts. (90, 104, 120 sts)

**Next row (WS):** K3, purl until 3 sts left, k3.

Rep Raglan Inc row 7 (8, 9) more times,

ending with a RS row. (146, 168, 192 sts)

*At the same time*, make 1 buttonhole at right front garter border on first (2nd, 2nd), then on 4th (5th, 5th), and on 7th (8th, 8th) Raglan Inc rows as follows: K1, yo, k2tog.

### Body

**Next row (WS):** Removing markers, k3, p19 (23, 27), sl next 30 (33, 39) sleeve sts to waste yarn, cable cast on 5 (7, 6) underarm sts, p42 (50, 54), sl sleeve sts to waste yarn, cable cast on 5 (7, 6) underarm sts, p19 (23, 27), k3. (96, 116, 126 sts)

**Next row (RS):** K3, work Row 1 of Lace pat to last 3 sts, k3.

Maintaining 3-st garter border, work even in Lace pat until body measures approx 6¼ (7½, 7½) inches, or ½ inch less than desired length from underarm, ending with Row 8 or 16 of pat.

Knit 6 rows.

Bind off all sts loosely.

### Sleeves

Pick up and knit 3 sts from underarm, pm for beg of rnd, pick up and knit 2 (4, 3) underarm sts, sl sts from waste yarn to dpns and knit to end of rnd. (35, 40, 45 sts)

Continue working Lace pat in the rnd, and work even for approx 5¾ (7, 8) inches, or ½ inch less than desired length from underarm, ending with Rnd 8 or 16 of pat.

[Knit 1 rnd, purl 1 rnd] 3 times.

Bind off all sts loosely.

Rep for other sleeve.

### Finishing
### Neck edging
With RS facing, pick up and knit 59 (65, 73) sts around neck edge.

**Row 1 (WS):** P1, *k1, p1, rep from * to end.

**Row 2:** Work in rib as established.

**Row 3:** Work in rib to last 3 sts, p2tog, yo, p1.

**Rows 4 and 5:** Work in rib as established.

Bind off very loosely in rib.

### Front edging
**Row 1:** With RS facing and using crochet hook, work 1 row of sc along the right front. Do not turn.

**Row 2 (RS):** Work rev sc along the edge. Fasten off.

Rep on left front.

Block to finished measurements.

Sew buttons to left front opposite buttonholes.

### Hat
With 2 dpn, cast on 3 sts.

Work I-cord as follows: *K3, do not turn, sl sts back to LH needle; rep from * for 15 rows.

Beg working in rnds.

**Rnd 1:** Knit in front and back of the each st and sl 2 sts to each of 3 needles, pm for beg of rnd and join. (6 sts)

continued on 169

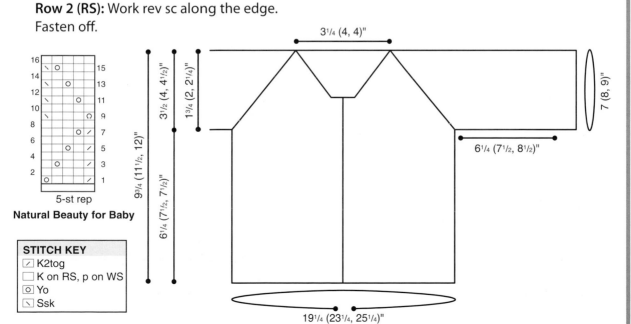

**Natural Beauty for Baby**

5-st rep

**STITCH KEY**
☐ K2tog (⊿)
☐ K on RS, p on WS
☐ Yo (○)
☐ Ssk (◣)

3¼ (4, 4)"

3½ (4, 4½)"

1¾ (2, 2¼)"

7 (8, 9)"

6¼ (7½, 8½)"

9¾ (11½, 12)"

6¼ (7½, 7½)"

19¼ (23¼, 25¼)"

# baby goes visiting

Design by Pauline Schultz

Dress Baby in this cozy poncho, romper pants and hat for an oh-so-cute picture-perfect look.

## Skill Level

◼◼◼◻ INTERMEDIATE

## Sizes

Infant 6 (12, 18) months Instructions are given for smallest size, with larger sizes in parentheses. When only 1 number is given, it applies to all sizes.

## Finished Measurements

**Poncho**
**Length:** 9½ (10¾, 12½) inches (excluding collar)
**Romper Pants**
**Waist:** 18½ (20, 21½) inches, adjustable with elastic
**Length:** 14 (14¾, 16½) inches
**Tam**
**Head circumference:** 15 (16, 17) inches

## Materials

▼ **Poncho and Tam:** Bernat Satin Sport Ombre 100 percent acrylic light weight yarn (182 yds/70g per ball): 2 (2, 2) balls seashore #04012 (A)
▼ **Romper Pants:** Bernat Satin Sport Solid 100 percent acrylic light weight yarn (221 yds/85g per ball): 1 (1, 2) balls taupe #03011 (B)

▼ Size 6 (4mm) double-point, 16- and 24-inch circular needles or size needed to obtain gauge
▼ Stitch markers, 1 in CC for beg of rnd
▼ 5 (¼-inch) pearl buttons
▼ 1½ yds (½-inch-wide) elastic for waist and ankle bands
▼ Tapestry needle
▼ Waste yarn

## Gauge

20 sts and 28 rows/rnds = 4 inches/10cm in St st
To save time, take time to check gauge.

## Special Abbreviations

**Inc1 (Increase 1):** On RS, knit into the front and back of st; on WS, purl into the front and back of next st
**CDD (Centered Double Decrease):** Sl 2 tog knitwise, k1, p2sso.

## Special Technique

**Provisional Cast On:** With crochet hook and waste yarn, make a chain several sts longer than desired cast on. With knitting needle and project yarn, pick up indicated number of sts in the "bumps" on back of chain. When indicated in pat, "unzip" the crochet chain to free live sts.

## Poncho

Using provisional cast on and A, cast on 41 (45, 49) sts; do not join.

**Row 1 (RS):** K3, *place marker, k8 (9, 10); rep from * 3 times, place marker, k3.

**Row 2:** K3, purl to last 3 sts, k3.

**Row 3 (inc):** K3, sl marker, Inc1, *knit to 1 st before marker, Inc1, sl marker, k1, Inc1; rep from * twice, knit to 2 sts before marker, Inc1, k1, sl marker, k3. (49, 53, 57 sts)

**Row 4:** K3, purl to last 3 sts, k3.

Rep [Rows 3 and 4] 8 (9, 10) times and on last row, remove 2nd and 4th markers at shoulders. (113, 125, 137 sts)

**Inc row (RS):** K3, sl marker, Inc1, knit to 1 st before marker at center back, Inc1, sl marker, k1, Inc1, knit to 2 sts before marker, Inc1, k1, sl marker, k3. (117, 129, 141 sts)

Maintaining 3-st garter edges, rep Inc row [every other row] 11 (13, 15) times, then [every 4th row] 4 (5, 6) times. (177, 201, 225 sts)

Work 2 rows even.

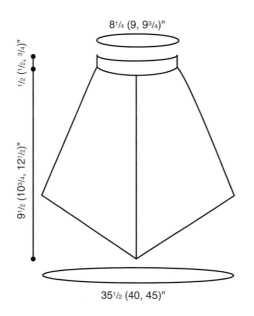

8¼ (9, 9¾)"

½ (½, ¾)"

9½ (10¾, 12½)"

35½ (40, 45)"

Maintaining 3-st garter edges, work K1, P1 Rib for 4 (4, 6) rows.

Bind off in pat.

## Collar

With RS facing, unzip crochet chain and sl 41 (45, 49) live sts to needle.

Work in K1, P1 rib for 7 (9, 11) rows.

Turn top of collar to WS and whipstitch live sts to first row of rib.

## Finishing

Sew 5 buttons evenly spaced on left front for boy *or* right front for girl.

Poke buttons through center of garter border on opposite front.

## Tam

With dpns and A, cast on 8 sts; distribute evenly over 4 dpns, place marker and join.

Knit 1 rnd.

**Next rnd:** Inc1 around. (16 sts)

**Rnd 1:** *K1, Inc1; rep from * around. (24 sts)

**Rnd 2:** Knit.

**Rnd 3:** *K2, Inc1; rep from * around. (32 sts)

**Rnd 4:** Knit.

Continue to inc every other rnd in this manner, knitting 1 more st before inc until there are 13 (14, 16) sts before the inc and on last rnd, shift beg of rnd marker back 6 sts. (120, 128, 152 sts)

**Dec rnd:** Placing double dec above inc on previous rnds, k6 (7, 9), CDD, *k12 (13, 15), CDD; rep from *, knit to end of rnd. (104, 112, 136 sts)

Rep Dec rnd [every other rnd] 3 (3, 4) more

times, working 2 fewer sts before the dec on each succeeding dec rnd. (56, 64, 72 sts)

Work 6 (6, 8) rnds in K1, P1 rib.

Bind off in rib.

Weave in all ends.

Block.

### Pompom

Cut 2 cardboard circles approx 4 inches in diameter. Cut a hole in the center of each circle, about ½-inch in diameter. Thread a tapestry needle with a length of yarn doubled. Holding both circles tog, insert needle through center hole, over the outside edge, through center again (Fig. 1) until entire circle is covered and center hole is filled (thread more length of yarn as needed).

times (Fig. 3) to prevent knot from slipping, pull tightly and tie into a firm knot. Remove cardboard and fluff out pompom by rolling it between your hands. Trim even with scissors, leaving tying ends for attaching pompom to project.

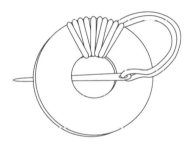

**Fig. 1**

With sharp scissors, cut yarn between the 2 circles all around the circumference (Fig. 2).

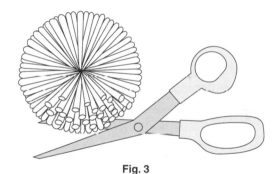

**Fig. 3**

Sew pompom to top center.

### Romper

Using provisional cast on with shorter circular needle and B, cast on 92 (100, 108) sts; do not join.

Work 8 rows in St st.

Purl 1 row (turning row), place marker for beg of rnd and join.

Knit 7 rnds.

**Next rnd (inc):** K14 (15, 16), Inc1, k13 (15, 17), Inc1, k14 (15, 16), Inc1, k1, Inc1, k14 (15, 16),

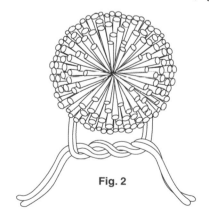

**Fig. 2**

Using 2 (12-inch) strands of yarn, sl yarn between circles and overlap yarn ends 2 or 3

Inc1, k13 (15, 17), Inc1, k14 (15, 16), Inc1, k1, Inc1. (100, 108, 116 sts)

Knit 7 (7, 9) rnds even.

**Next rnd (inc):** K14 (15, 16), Inc1, k15 (17, 19), Inc1, k15 (16, 17), Inc1, k1, Inc1, k15 (16, 17), Inc1, k16 (17, 19), Inc1, k15 (16, 17), [Inc1, k1] twice. (108, 116, 124 sts)

Knit 22 (26, 29) rnds.

## Beg crotch shaping
**Next rnd:** Mark center front and back as follows: k27 (29, 31), place marker, k54 (58, 62), place marker, knit to end of rnd.

**Inc rnd:** *Knit to 2 sts before front marker, Inc1, k1, sl marker, Inc1; rep from * for back marker, then knit to end of rnd. (112, 120, 128 sts)

Rep Inc rnd [every other rnd] 2 (2, 3) times, then [every rnd] 3 (3, 4) times. (132, 140, 156 sts)

## Divide for legs
**Next rnd:** Removing markers, work to first marker, sl next 66 (70, 78) sts to waste yarn for holder.

### First Leg
Sl rem 66 (70, 78) sts to dpns, with yarn at center crotch.

**Rnd 1:** Turn and cable cast on 3 sts, place marker for center crotch and new beg of rnd, cable cast on 3 sts, turn and knit to end of rnd. (72, 76, 84 sts)

**Dec rnd:** K1, k2tog, knit to last 3 sts, ssk, k1. (70, 74, 82 sts)

Rep Dec rnd [every rnd] 7 (8, 9) times, then [every other rnd] 2 (3, 4) times. (52, 52, 56 sts)

Work even until leg measures 6½ (6¾, 7¼) inches or ¾ inch less than desired length.

**Next rnd:** K2tog around.

Knit 4 rnds, purl 1 rnd.

Remove marker and beg working back and forth.

Knit 1 row, purl 1 row, knit 1 row.

Sl sts to waste yarn.

Fold leg sts at turning rnd and whipstitch sts to WS of dec rnd.

### Second Leg
Sl 2nd leg sts from waste yarn to dpns.

**Rnd 1:** With RS facing and beg at center crotch, pick up and knit 3 sts from crotch, knit to end, then pick up and knit 3 sts from crotch; place marker for center crotch and beg of rnd.

Continue as for first leg.

## Finishing
Weave in all ends. Block to finished measurements.

Unzip waist edge cast on and sl live sts to circular needle.

Fold at turning row and neatly whipstitch live sts to WS.

Thread elastic through waist and ankles, then sew ends of elastic tog. ▼

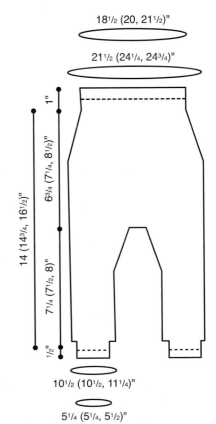

# busy day dress

**Design by Joyce Nordstrom**

Playful children will enjoy wearing this clever knit dress alone or over a T-shirt—it's simply darling.

## Skill Level

 EASY

## Sizes

Child's sizes 2 (6) Instructions are given for smallest size, with larger size in parentheses. When only 1 number is given, it applies to both sizes.

## Finished Measurements

**Chest:** 22½ (26½) inches
**Length:** 16 (17½) inches

## Materials

▼ Moda Dea Sassy Stripes 100 percent acrylic light weight yarn (147 yd/50g per ball): 3 (4) balls vintage #6935
▼ Size 4 (3.5mm) double-pointed needles
▼ Size 6 (4mm) 24-inch circular needle or size needed to obtain gauge
▼ Stitch markers, 1 in CC for beg of rnd
▼ Tapestry needle
▼ Waste yarn

## Gauge

20 sts and 28 rows = 4 inches/10cm in St st with larger needles
To save time, take time to check gauge.

## Pattern Note

Sundress is worked from shoulders down to underarms; front and back are then joined and worked in the rnd to bottom.

## Back Yoke

With larger circular needle, cast on 40 (48) sts. Do not join.

Work even in St st for 3½ (4) inches, ending with a WS row.

Inc 1 st at each armhole edge on next, then [every other row] 1 (2) more time(s), ending with a WS row. (44, 54 sts)

Cast on 2 sts at beg of next 6 rows. (56, 66 sts)

Sl all sts to waste yarn.

## Front Yoke & Neck

With RS facing and using larger needle, pick up and knit 10 (12) sts along cast-on edge of back; skip center 20 (24) back neck sts; with 2nd ball, pick up and knit rem 10 (12) sts.

Working both sides at once with separate balls of yarn, work 3 rows of St st.

Inc 1 st at each neck edge [every RS row] 7 (9) times, ending with a WS row. (17, 21 sts on each side)

Cut yarn on left front.

Work across right front sts, cast on 6 sts, then work across left front sts. (40, 48 sts)

Work even until front measures 3½ (4) inches, ending with a WS row.

Inc 1 st at each armhole edge on next, then [every other row] 1 (2) more time(s), ending with a WS row. (44, 54 sts)

Cast on 2 sts at beg of next 6 rows. (56, 66 sts)

## Body

**Rnd 1 (RS):** Knit across front sts, place marker, sl back sts from waste yarn to LH needle and knit across, place marker for beg of rnd and join. (112, 132 sts)

Knit 8 rnds even.

**Inc rnd:** *K1, M1, knit to 1 st before marker, M1, k1, sl marker; rep from * to end of rnd. (116, 136 sts)

Rep Inc rnd [every 9th rnd] 6 (7) times. (140, 164 sts)

Work even until body measures approx 10 (10¾) inches from armholes or 1 inch short of desired length.

Work in K2, P2 Rib for 1 inch.

Bind off loosely in rib.

## Finishing
### Armhole edging
With RS facing, using smaller dpns and beg at center underarm, pick up and knit 56 (60) sts around armhole edge, place marker for beg of rnd and join.

Work 4 rnds in K2, P2 Rib.

Bind off very loosely in rib.

### Neck edging
With RS facing and using dpns, pick up and knit 60 (68) sts around neck edge.

Work as for armhole edging.

Weave in all ends. Block to finished measurements. ▼

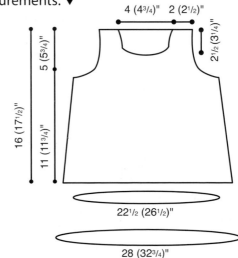

# ahoy little mate!

Design by Joyce Nordstrom

Your precious baby will sail through a busy schedule in this delightful sweater and hat set.

## Skill Level
●■■■□ INTERMEDIATE

## Sizes
Newborn (6 months, 12 months) Instructions are given for smallest size, with larger sizes in parentheses. When only 1 number is given, it applies to all sizes.

## Finished Measurements
**Chest:** 20¼ (21¼, 22½) inches (buttoned)
**Length:** 9¾ (9¾, 10) inches (excluding collar)

## Materials
▼ TLC Cotton Plus 51 percent cotton/49 percent acrylic medium weight yarn (178 yds/100g per skein): 2 (2, 3) skeins white #3001 (MC) and 1 skein red #3907 (CC)
▼ Size 5 (3.75mm) double-pointed and 24-inch circular needles
▼ Size 7 (4.5mm) double-pointed and 24-inch circular needles or size needed to obtain gauge
▼ 3 (⅞-inch) buttons
▼ Waste yarn

## Gauge
20 sts and 25 rows = 4 inches/10cm with larger needle.
To save time, take time to check gauge.

## Special Technique
**3-Needle Bind Off:** With RS tog and needles parallel, using a 3rd needle, knit tog a st from the front needle with a st from the back. *Knit tog a st from the front and back needles, and sl the first st over the 2nd to bind off. Rep from * across, then fasten off last st.

## Pattern Notes
The sweater is worked from shoulders down to underarms; then the body is joined and worked in 1 piece to bottom; front neck shaping continues after the join. The sleeves are worked in the rnd from the armhole edge down.

The shawl sailor collar is sewn on so that the RS of back flap hangs over back sweater. The cap is worked back and forth from lower edge.

## Sweater
### Back Yoke
With larger needle and MC, cast on 50 (53, 56) sts.

Work in St st for 4 (4¼, 4½) inches, ending with WS row.

Place all sts on waste yarn.

### Front Yokes
With RS facing, using larger needle and MC, pick up and knit 16 (17, 18) sts along cast-on edge of back; skip center 18 (19, 20) back neck sts; with 2nd ball of MC, pick up and knit rem 16 (17, 18) sts.

Working both sides at once in St st with separate balls of yarn, inc 1 st at each neck edge [every other row] 2, (2, 3) times, then [every 4th row] 6 times. (24, 25, 27 sts each side)

### Body
*At the same time*, when fronts measure same as back, ending on a WS row, join pieces as follows: knit across right front, sl back sts from waste yarn to LH needle and knit across, knit across left front.

When neck inc are complete, ending with a WS row, cast on 4 sts at each neck edge. (106, 111, 118 sts)

Working 4 edge sts each side in garter st and rest of body in St st, work even for ½ inch.

**Buttonhole row:** Working in pat as established, make a buttonhole in the 4 right front edge sts (girl) or left front edge sts (boy) as follows: k1, k2tog, yo, k1.

Work even for 2 inches, then rep Buttonhole row.

Work even for 1 inch, ending with a RS row.

**Next row (WS):** Purl, dec 5 (7, 9) sts evenly spaced across. (101, 104, 109 sts)

### Bottom ribbing
Change to smaller needle.

**Row 1 (RS):** With MC, k4, *p1, k1; rep from * to last 5 sts, p1, k4.

**Row 2:** With MC, *k4, *k1, p1; rep from * to last 5 sts, k5.

Continue in pat as established for 8 more rows, alternating 2 rows CC, 2 rows MC, and placing 3rd buttonhole in next MC row.

With MC, bind off loosely in rib.

### Sleeves
With RS facing, using larger dpns and MC and beg at center underarm, pick up and knit 41 (43, 45) sts around armhole, place marker for beg of rnd and join.

Knit 1 rnd.

**Dec rnd:** K1, k2tog, knit to last 2 sts, ssk. (39, 41, 43 sts)

Continue in St st and rep Dec rnd [every 4th rnd] 5 (6, 7) times. (29 sts)

Work even until sleeve measures 5½ (5¾, 6) inches, or 1¾ inches less than desired length.

**Next rnd:** Knit and dec 1 st.

## Cuff
**Rnds 1 and 2:** With MC, *k1, p1; rep from * around.

Continue in rib as established for 8 more rnds, alternating 2 rnds CC, 2 rnds MC.

With MC, bind off loosely in rib.

## Collar
With larger needle and MC, cast on 42 (43, 46) sts.

Knit 3 rows with MC, *knit 2 rows with CC, knit 2 rows with MC; rep from * once.

Keeping 4 sts each side of collar in garter st, work rem sts in St st until piece measures 4 inches from beg, ending with WS row.

**Next row (RS):** Work across 12 (12, 13) sts, bind off 18 (19, 20) sts; attach another ball of yarn and work across rem 12, (12, 13) sts.

Working both sides at once with separate balls of yarn, dec at neck edge [every other row] 2 (2, 3) times, then [every 4th row] 6 times. (4 sts rem each side)

Bind off.

## Finishing
With RS of collar and WS of sweater facing and using mattress st, sew collar to sweater, aligning backs of neck tog and matching inc of fronts to dec of collar.

Sew 4 garter sts on collar to 4 band sts on fronts.

Turn collar so RS of collar is on outside.

Weave in all ends. Block to finished measurements. Sew buttons opposite buttonholes.

## Cap
With smaller needle and MC, cast on 61 (65, 69) sts; do not join.

**Row 1:** K4, *p1, k1; rep from * to last 5 sts, p1, k4.

**Row 2:** K4, *k1, p1; rep from * to last 5 sts, k5.

Rep Rows 1 and 2 with [2 rows CC, 2 rows MC] twice.

Change to larger needle and

**continued on 169**

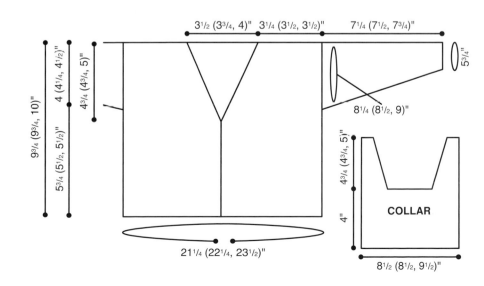

# classy unisex cardigan

Design by Debbie O'Neill

This toddler cardigan has a fun ribbing and is perfect for any occasion.

## Skill Level

■■□□□ EASY

## Sizes

Child's 12 months (2 years, 4 years) Instructions are given for smallest size, with larger sizes in parentheses. When only 1 number is given, it applies to all sizes.

## Finished Measurements

**Chest:** 24 (26¼, 28¾) inches (buttoned)
**Length:** 13 (14, 16) inches

## Materials

▼ Plymouth/Cleckheaton Country 8 Ply 100 percent superwash wool light weight yarn (105 yds/50g per ball): 4 (5, 7) balls lime green #2250
▼ Size 6 double-pointed and 24-inch circular needles or size needed to obtain gauge
▼ Stitch markers
▼ Waste yarn
▼ Tapestry needle
▼ 5 (⅝-inch) buttons

## Gauge

22 sts and 30 rows = 4 inches/10cm in St st
To save time, take time to check gauge.

## Special Abbreviations

**RT (Right Twist):** K2tog, leaving sts on LH needle; insert RH needle from the front between the 2 sts just knitted tog, and knit the first st again; sl both sts from the needle.
**Pm:** Place marker.

## Pattern Stitches

**A. Herringbone Rib** (worked in rows on a multiple of 9 sts + 3)
**Row 1 (RS):** *P3, [RT] 3 times; rep from * to last 3 sts, p3.
**Row 2:** *K3, p6; rep from * to last 3 sts, k3.
**Row 3:** * P3, k1, [RT] twice, k1; rep from * to last 3 sts, p3.
**Row 4:** Rep Row 2.
Rep Rows 1–4 for pat.

**B. Herringbone Rib** (worked in rnds on a multiple of 9 sts)
**Rnd 1:** *P3, [RT] 3 times; rep from * around.
**Rnd 2:** *P3, k6; rep from * around.
**Rnd 3:** *P3, k1, [RT] twice, k1; rep from * around.
**Rnd 4:** Rep Rnd 2.
Rep Rnds 1–4 for pat.

## Pattern Notes

Cardigan is worked with raglan shaping;

when yoke is complete, the body is joined and worked to the lower edge; the sleeves are worked in the rnd from the underarm to cuff.

The yoke and lower body are all worked back and forth; a circular needle is used to accommodate the large number of sts.

### Yoke
With circular needle, cast on 36 (38, 40) sts.

**Row 1 (WS):** Purl, placing markers as follows: 1 front st, pm, 1 raglan seam st, pm, 6 sleeve sts, pm, 1 raglan seam st, pm, 18 (20, 22) back sts, pm, 1 raglan seam st, pm, 6 sleeve sts, pm, 1 raglan seam st, pm, 1 front st.

### Begin Raglan
**Inc row 1 (RS):** *Knit to marker, M1, sl marker, k1, sl marker, M1; rep from * across, then knit to end. (44, 46, 48 sts)

Continue in St st and rep Inc row 1 [every other row] twice more, ending with a WS row. (60, 62, 64 sts)

### Shape neck
**Inc row 2 (RS):** K1, M1, *knit to marker, M1, sl marker, k1, sl marker, M1; rep from * across, then knit to last st, M1, K1. (70, 72, 74 sts)

Rep Inc row 2 [every other row] 5 (6, 7) times more. (120, 132, 144 sts on the needle)

**Next row (WS):** Purl to end of row, then cast on 2 sts. (122, 134, 146 sts)

**Next row:** Rep Inc row 1, then cast on 2 sts. (132, 144, 156 sts)

Continue in St st and rep Inc row 1 [every other row] 9 (10, 11) times, ending with a WS row. (212, 232, 252 sts)

## Separate sections

Removing markers, knit across right front, sl next 48 (52, 56) sts to waste yarn for sleeve, cast on 6 (6, 7) sts for underarm, knit across back sts, sl next 48 (52, 56) sts to waste yarn for sleeve, cast on 6 (6, 7) sts for underarm, knit left front. (128, 140, 154 sts)

## Body

Work even in St st for 5¼ (5¾, 7) inches
or
2½ inches less than desired length, ending with a RS row.

**Next row (WS):** Inc 1 (dec 2, inc 2) sts, placing inc/dec at underarm(s). (129, 138, 156 sts)

Work Herringbone Rib pat for 2½ inches.

Bind off loosely in rib.

## Sleeves

Sl sleeve sts to dpns.

With RS facing and beg at center underarm, pick up and knit 3 (3, 4) sts, knit sleeve sts, pick up and knit 3 sts, pm for beg of rnd and join. (54, 58, 63 sts)

Work even in St st for approx 1 inch.

**Dec rnd:** K1, k2tog, knit to last 2 sts, ssk. (52, 56, 61 sts)

Continue in St st and rep Dec rnd [every 4th rnd] 8 (10, 8) times. (36, 36, 45 sts)

Work even until sleeve measures 6 (7, 8) inches from underarm, or 2½ inches less than desired length.

Work Herringbone Rib pat for 2½ inches.

Bind off loosely in rib.

## Finishing
## Button band

***Note:*** *Button band is worked on left front for girl's sweater, right front for boy's.*

With RS facing and using circular needle, pick up and knit approx 54 (62, 70) sts along front edge.

Knit 6 rows.

Bind off.

## Buttonhole band

***Note:*** *Buttonhole band is worked on right front for girl's sweater, left front for boy's.*

Place 5 markers evenly spaced between lower edge and neck edge of front.

With RS facing and using circular needle, pick up and knit approx 54 (62, 70) sts along front edge.

Knit 3 rows.

**Next row:** Knit across and bind off 2 sts for buttonholes at each marker.

**Next row:** Knit across and cast on 2 sts

above each set of bound-off sts.

Knit 1 row.

Bind off all sts.

### Neck edging
With RS facing and using circular needle, pick up and knit approx 72 (80, 88) sts around the neck.

Knit 2 rows.

Bind off all sts.

Weave in all ends. Block to finished measurements. Sew on buttons opposite buttonholes. ▼

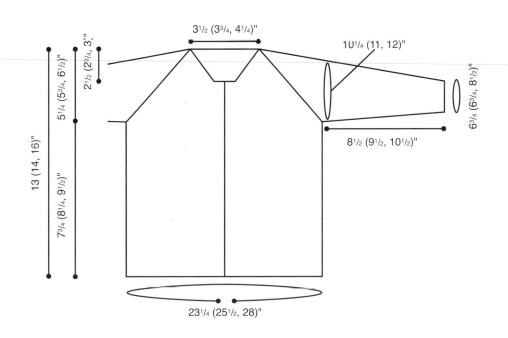

# hats & socks

These projects offer

needed warmth

for everyone in a

variety of looks for

great gift giving.

# making news cap

Design by Phoenix Bess

Dress up this sporty style with a rhinestone buckle and print ribbon, or choose more rustic trimmings.

## Skill Level
■■■□ INTERMEDIATE

## Sizes
Medium (large) Instructions are given for smaller size, with larger size in parentheses. When only 1 number is given, it applies to both sizes.

## Finished Measurement
**Hatband Circumference:** 20 (22) inches

## Materials
▼ Berroco Suede 100 percent nylon medium weight yarn (120 yds/50g per ball): 3 balls Wild Bill Hickcock #3717
▼ Size 7 (4.5mm) double-pointed, 16- and 24-inch circular needles or size needed to obtain gauge
▼ Medium-size crochet hook (for provisional cast-on)
▼ Waste yarn
▼ Tapestry needle
▼ 7-count plastic canvas
▼ 24-inches 1-inch-wide elastic
▼ 20 inches ⅞-inch-wide camel Wildcat grosgrain ribbon from Offray
▼ Aleene's Fabric Fusion adhesive

▼ 1⅛-inch silver-tone rhinestone buckle from Sunbelt Fastener Co.
▼ Sewing needle
▼ Thread to match yarn

## Gauge
19 sts and 28 rnds = 4 inches/10cm in St st
To save time, take time to check gauge.

## Special Abbreviations
**Inc1 (Increase 1):** Inc by knitting in front and back of st.
**W&T (Wrap and Turn):** Bring yarn to RS of work between needles, sl next st purlwise to RH needle, bring yarn around this st to WS, sl st back to LH needle, turn work to beg working back in the other direction.

## Special Techniques
**Provisional Cast On:** With crochet hook and waste yarn, make a chain several sts longer than desired cast on. With knitting needle and project yarn, pick up indicated number of sts in the "bumps" on back of chain. When indicated in pat, "unzip" the crochet chain to free live sts.
**Hiding wraps:** On RS rows: pick up wrap from front to back and knit tog with wrapped st. On WS rows: pick up wrap

from the back, then purl it tog with wrapped st.

## Pattern Notes
The top of the hat is a basic circular spiral made by inc 8 sts every other rnd, with 1 more st between the inc on each succeeding inc rnd. The inc rnds may be worked until you have reached the circumference of your choosing, allowing you to customize the fullness of the top of your hat. The top of the model shown has a 46-inch circumference before it is gathered into the band. To make a less full hat, dec circumference by eliminating inc rnds; for additional fullness, work more inc rnds.

Change from dpns to circular needle when there are enough sts to fit comfortably on the needle.

## Top of Hat
Make a sl knot, being sure that the short tail is the end to pull to tighten the knot.

[Yo, knit into sl knot] 4 times. (8 sts)

Distribute sts onto 4 dpns (2 on each), place marker for beg of rnd and join, taking care not to twist sts.

**Rnd 1:** Inc1 around. (16 sts)

**Rnds 2 and 4:** Knit.

**Rnd 3:** *Inc1, k1, place marker; rep from * around. (24 sts)

**Rnd 5:** *Inc1, knit to marker; rep from * around. (32 sts)

**Rnd 6:** Knit.

Rep Rnds 5 and 6 until there are 27 sts between markers. (216 sts)

Bind off very loosely.

## Hatband
With 16-inch circular needle, cast on 95 (104) sts; place marker and join, taking care not to twist sts.

Knit 9 rnds.

**Next rnd:** Bind off 54 sts, cast on 54 sts, then purl rem sts for turning ridge.

Knit 9 rnds.

Bind off.

## Brim
### First Half
Using Provisional Cast On method, cast on 54 sts; do not join.

Knit 3 rows.

### Short-row shaping
**Row 1 (WS):** P30, W&T.

**Row 2 (RS):** K9, W&T.

**Row 3:** P12, hiding up wrap when you come to it, W&T.

Continue in this manner, working 3 sts past previously wrapped st until all sts have been worked.

Knit 1 row.

Bind off.

### Second Half
Undo provisional cast on and sl live sts to needle.

Beg with Row 1 of Short Row Shaping, work 2nd half of brim as for first half.

## Finishing
With yarn and tapestry needle, make a running st through every other st around

entire bound-off edge of top of hat. Pull on both ends of yarn to gather the edge until the circumference is same as hatband. Secure gather by whipstitching around edge.

Use whipstitch to attach cast-on edge of hat band to gathered edge of hat.

Cut a piece of plastic embroidery canvas to fit hat brim and slide into brim. Remember that the front of your head curves, so the edge facing your head will need to be curved slightly. Try on hat to check fit of brim against your forehead and trim until brim fits properly.

With RS facing and using invisible seam method, sew brim to open slit in hat band, avoiding any puckering along the join.

Fold the band at turning ridge and whipstitch bound-off edge of band to WS of top to form casing for elastic; leave a couple inches open to insert elastic.

Thread elastic through the casing. Try on the hat; adjust elastic as necessary for fit; tack ends of elastic tog and finish sewing casing closed.

Cut ribbon to 15 inches (or length necessary to span the width between the ends of the brim). Dip ends of ribbon in fabric glue to prevent fraying. Slide buckle onto ribbon and position 3½ inches from end of ribbon on RH side of hat (wearing it). Carefully cut a tiny slit for the buckle prong, coat slit with fabric glue to prevent fraying and push prong through slit. Tack ends of ribbon to band with sewing thread.

Weave in all ends. ▼

# the warm button set

Designs by Kathy Sasser

There's a button on the hat to slip into a buttonhole on the scarf—the better to keep your neck warm and chill-free!

## Skill Level
◼◼◻◻ EASY

## Sizes
Small (medium, large) Instructions are for smallest size with larger sizes in parentheses. When only 1 number is given it applies to all sizes.

## Finished Measurements
**Hat circumference:** 21 (22, 23) inches
**Scarf:** 7 x 72 inches

## Materials
▼ Lion Brand Vanna's Choice 100 percent acrylic medium weight yarn (170 yds/100g per ball): 4 (4, 5) balls mustard #158
▼ Size 6 (4mm) double-pointed and 16-inch circular needles
▼ Size 7 (4.5mm) 16-, 24- and 29-inch circular needles or size needed to obtain gauge
▼ Tapestry needle
▼ ⅞-inch button
▼ Safety pin or marker

## Gauge
20 sts and 26 rows (rnds) = 4 inches/10cm in St st with larger needles
To save time, take time to check gauge.

## Hat
Cut 1 (60-inch) length of yarn and set aside.

With larger 16-inch circular needle, loosely cast on 53 (55, 57) sts; place marker for beg of rnd and join, being careful not to twist sts.

Knit 6 rnds.

Thread tapestry needle with 60-inch length, folding in half to form a double thickness. Leaving sts on circular needle, insert tapestry needle purlwise through each st, then remove tapestry needle, leaving cut length in place.

Knit 1 rnd.

**Inc rnd:** Knit in front and back of each st and mark this rnd with safety pin or other marker. (106, 110, 114 sts)

## Scarf

With 29-inch needle, cast on 363 sts. Do not join.

Beg with a RS row, work in St st for 4 rows.

**Buttonhole row:** K180, bind off 3 sts, then knit to end of row.

**Next row:** Purl to 3 bound-off sts, cast on 3 sts, then purl to end of row.

Work even until piece measures 7 inches from beg.

Bind off evenly.

### 2-stitch I-Cord Fringe

Pick up and knit 2 sts at corner of short edge of scarf; *do not turn, sl sts back to LH needle, k2; rep from * until cord measures approx 5 inches or desired length. Bind off.

Referring to photo for placement, rep for each I-Cord Fringe across short edge, then across opposite short edge, varying length of fringes as desired.

### Finishing

Allow edges to roll. Weave in all loose ends. ▼

Work even in St st until hat measures 5¾ (6¼, 6¾) inches from safety pin.

Change to smaller needle and work K1, P1 Rib for 6 inches.

Bind off loosely.

### Finishing

Gather top of hat by pulling ends of yarn threaded through sts at top tightly tog and tie with a secure knot. Bring ends to WS and knot again, then cut.

Fold brim in half and sew bound-off edge to WS at beg of rib.

Sew button to outside of hat, ½-inch from bottom edge. Button will mark center back of hat.

Weave in loose ends. Block as necessary.

# quick unisex hats

**Design by Cecily Glowik**

Start at the top and end with earflaps using chunky yarn in colorful prints or sensible solid shades.

### Skill Level

 EASY

### Sizes

Woman's (Man's) Instructions are given for smaller size, with larger size in parentheses. When only 1 number is given, it applies to both sizes.

### Finished Measurements

**Fits head circumference:** 20 (22) inches

### Materials

- ▼ N.Y. Yarns Action 70 percent acrylic/30 percent wool super bulky weight yarn (49 yds/50g per ball): 2 balls pastels #03 [woman's hat]
- ▼ Classic Elite Aspen 50 percent alpaca/50 percent wool super bulky weight yarn (51 yds/100g per skein): 2 skeins starry night #1510 [man's hat]
- ▼ Size 17 (12.75mm) double-pointed and 16-inch circular needles (optional) or size needed to obtain gauge
- ▼ Stitch marker
- ▼ Tapestry needle

**6 SUPER BULKY**

## Gauge
8 sts and 10 rnds = 4 inches/10cm in St st
To save time, take time to check gauge.

## Special Abbreviation
**Inc1 (Increase 1):** Inc by knitting in front and back of st.
**M1 (Make 1):** Insert LH needle from front to back under the running thread between the last st worked and next st on LH. With RH needle, knit into the back of resulting lp.

## Special Technique
**I-Cord:** *Sl sts back to LH needle, k3, do not turn; rep from * until cord is desired length. Bind off.

## Pattern Stitch
**Seed St in the Rnd** (even number of sts)
**Rnd 1:** *K1, p1; rep from * around.
**Rnd 2:** *P1, k1; rep from * around.
Rep Rnds 1 and 2 for pat.

## Pattern Note
If desired, change to 16-inch circular needle when sts will fit comfortably on it.

## Hat
Cast on 3 sts onto 1 dpn, then distribute onto 3 dpns (1 st on each needle); place marker for beg of rnd and join, being careful not to twist sts.

**Rnd 1:** [Inc1] around. (6 sts)

**Rnds 2, 5, 7, 9:** Knit.

**Rnd 3:** *K1, M1, k1; rep from * around. (9 sts)

**Rnd 4:** *K1, M1, k1, m1, k1; rep from * around. (15 sts)

**Rnd 6:** *K2, M1; rep from* to last st, k1. (22 sts)

**Rnd 8:** *K3, M1; rep from * to last st, k1. (29 sts)

**Rnd 10:** *K4, M1; rep from * to last st, k1. (36 sts)

**Rnd 11:** Knit all sts.

**Rnd 12:** Inc 0 (4) sts evenly spaced around. (36, 40 sts)

**Rnds 13–18:** Knit.

**Rnds 19–24 (26):** Work in Seed St.

**Next rnd:** Bind off 3 (4) sts, k9 sts and sl sts to waste yarn for earflap, bind off 12 (14) sts, k9 sts and sl to waste yarn for 2nd earflap, bind off rem 3 (4) sts.

## Earflaps
Sl 9 sts from waste yarn to dpn and attach yarn with WS facing.

**Rows 1, 3 and 5 (WS):** Purl.

**Rows 2 and 4:** Sl 1, ssk, knit to last 3 sts, k2tog, sl 1. (5 sts)

**Row 6:** Sl 1, k3tog, sl 1, do not turn. (3 sts)

Work 3-st I-Cord for 7 inches.

K3tog and pull yarn through last st made.

Rep for 2nd earflap.

## Finishing
Weave in ends. Block lightly. ▼

# bavarian style

Design by Christine Walter

Start at the top and use twisted stitches to add interest all around this fashion-savvy wool hat.

## Skill Level
■■■□ INTERMEDIATE

## Size
Fits head circumference of 20–22 inches

## Materials
▼ Berroco Pure Merino 100 percent extra-fine merino wool medium weight yarn (92 yds/50g per ball): 2 balls cardinal #8555
▼ Size 7 (4.5mm) double-pointed needles (set of 5) or size needed to obtain gauge
▼ Stitch markers, 1 in CC for beg of rnd
▼ Tapestry needle

## Gauge
20 sts and 26 rnds = 4 inches/10 cm in Twisted St st
1 panel rep = 2½ inches/6.5cm wide
To save time, take time to check gauge

## Special Abbreviations
**Inc1 (Increase 1):** Inc by knitting into the back and front of st.
**LT (Left Twist):** Wyif, sl 2 sts purlwise to RH needle. Holding the LH needle in front of the work, skip the purl st and insert needle into the knit st. Draw out the RH needle, letting the purl st fall free. Pick it up from the back with the RH needle and sl it back to LH needle (sts have switched places). Work p1, k1-tbl.
**RT (Right Twist):** Wyib, sl 2 sts purlwise to the RH needle. From the back, insert LH needle into the purl st, draw out the RH needle, letting the twisted knit st fall free, then pick it up again with the RH needle from the front and sl it back to the LH needle (sts have switched places). Work k1-tbl, p1.

## Pattern Stitches
**A. Twisted St st (any number of sts)**
Knit all sts tbl on all rnds.
**B. Carved Diamond (multiple of 15 sts)**
**Rnds 1 and 2:** *K1-tbl, p3, k1-tbl, p2, k1-tbl, p2, k1-tbl, p3, k1-tbl; rep from * around.
**Rnd 3:** *K1-tbl, p2, RT, p2, k1-tbl, p2, LT, p2, k1-tbl; rep from * around.
**Rnd 4:** *K1-tbl, p1, RT, p3, k1-tbl, p3, LT, p1, k1-tbl; rep from * around.
**Rnd 5:** *K1-tbl, RT, p3, k3-tbl, p3, LT, k1-tbl; rep from * around.
**Rnd 6:** *K1-tbl, p4, RT, k1-tbl, LT, p4, k1-tbl; rep from * around.
**Rnd 7:** *K1-tbl, p3, RT, p1, k1-tbl, p1, LT, p3, k1-tbl; rep from * around.
**Rnd 8:** *K1-tbl, p2, RT, p1, k3-tbl, p1, LT, p2, k1-tbl; rep from * around.

**Rnd 9:** *K1-tbl, p1, RT, p1, RT, k1-tbl, LT, p1, LT, p1, k1-tbl; rep from * around.

**Rnd 10:** *K1-tbl, RT, p1, RT, p1, k1-tbl, p1, LT, p1, LT, k1-tbl; rep from * around.

**Rnd 11:** *K1-tbl, p2, RT, p2, k1-tbl, p2, LT, p2, k1-tbl; rep from * around.

**Rnds 12 and 13:** *K1-tbl, p2, k1-tbl, p3, k1-tbl, p3, k1-tbl, p2, k1-tbl; rep from * around.

**Rnd 14:** *K2-tbl, p1, LT, p2, k1-tbl, p2, RT, p1, k2-tbl; rep from * around.

**Rnd 15:** *K1-tbl, LT, p1, LT, p1, k1-tbl, p1, RT, p1, RT, k1-tbl; rep from * around.

**Rnd 16:** *K1-tbl, p1, LT, p1, LT, k1-tbl, RT, p1, RT, p1, k1-tbl; rep from * around.

**Rnd 17:** *K1-tbl, p2, LT, p2, k1-tbl, p2, RT, p2, k1-tbl; rep from * around.

**Rnd 18:** *K1-tbl, p3, LT, p1, k1-tbl, p1, RT, p3, k1-tbl; rep from * around.

**Rnd 19:** *K2-tbl, p3, LT, k1-tbl, RT, p3, k2-tbl; rep from * around.

**Rnd 20:** *K1-tbl, LT, p4, k1-tbl, p4, RT, k1-tbl; rep from * around.

**Rnd 21:** *K1-tbl, p1, LT, p3, k1-tbl, p3, RT, p1, k1-tbl; rep from * around.

**Rnd 22:** *K1-tbl, p2, LT, p2, k1-tbl, p2, RT, p2, k1-tbl; rep from * around.

### Pattern Note
If a fold over brim is desired, work more rnds of the ribbed edge.

### Hat
#### Crown
Cast on 4 sts and distribute on 4 dpns (1 on each needle); place marker for beg of rnd and join, being careful not to twist sts.

**Rnds 1 and 3:** Inc1 in each st around. (16 sts)

**Rnds 2, 4 and 6:** [K1-tbl] around.

**Rnd 5:** *Inc1, k1-tbl, place marker; rep from * around. (24 sts)

**Rnd 7:** *Inc1, knit all sts tbl to marker; rep from * around. (32 sts)

**Rnd 8:** [K1-tbl] around.

Rep Rnds 7 and 8 until there are 30 sts on each needle. (120 sts)

### Body
Work 22 rnds of Carved Diamond pat.

### Edging
**Rnd 1:** *[K1-tbl, p1] 7 times, k1-tbl; rep from * around.

Rep [Rnd 1] 9 more times or for desired length.

Bind off loosely in pat.

### Finishing
Weave in ends. Block as necessary. ▼

**STITCH KEY**
◇ K1-tbl
– Purl
⟋ RT
⟍ LT

15-st rep
**BAVARIAN STYLE**

# undulations socks

Design by Amy Polcyn

Use a fingering weight for these easy-to-make, perfect-fit socks for any size!

## Skill Level

INTERMEDIATE

## Sizes

Woman's small (medium, large, extra-large) to fit shoe sizes 6/6½ (7/7½, 8/8½, 9/9½)

Instructions are given for smallest size, with larger sizes in parentheses. When only 1 number is given, it applies to all sizes. When 2 numbers are given, the smaller is for a narrow/medium foot and the larger is for a wider foot.

## Finished Measurements

**Length:** 8¾ (9, 9¼, 9¾) inches

**Circumference:** 8 (9½) inches

## Materials

- South West Trading Co. TOFUtsies 50 percent superwash wool/25 percent Soysilk™/22½ percent cotton/2½ percent chitin superfine weight yarn (465 yds/100g per ball): 1 ball light foot #730 (1 SUPER FINE)
- Size 1 (2.5mm) double-pointed needles (set of 5) or size needed to obtain gauge
- Small crochet hook
- Spare needle 1 or 2 sizes larger
- Waste yarn
- Stitch marker
- Tapestry needle

## Gauge

30 sts and 46 rows = 4 inches/10cm in St st

To save time, take time to check gauge.

## Special Abbreviations

**N1, N2, N3, N4:** Needles 1, 2, 3, 4.

## Special Techniques

**Provisional Cast On:** With crochet hook and waste yarn, make a chain several sts longer than desired cast on. With knitting needle and project yarn, pick up indicated number

of sts in the "bumps" on back of chain. When indicated in pat, "unzip" the crochet chain to free live sts.

**Wrap and Turn:** Move yarn between needles to RS, sl next st, move yarn back to WS, turn piece, sl st back to other needle.

## Pattern Stitch
**Undulation Pat (multiple of 6 sts)**
**Rnds 1 and 2:** *P4, k2; rep from * to end.
**Rnds 3 and 4:** *P3, k3; rep from * to end.
**Rnds 5 and 6:** *P2, k4; rep from * to end.
**Rnds 7 and 8:** *P1, k4, p1; rep from * to end.
**Rnds 9 and 10:** *P1, k3, p2; rep from * to end.
**Rnds 11 and 12:** *P1, k2, p3; rep from * to end.
Rep Rnds 1–12 for pat.

## Pattern Notes
Work length appropriate for shoe size. Smaller st count is for narrow/medium width foot; larger st count is for wide foot.

Sock circumference should be approximately 10 percent less than actual foot measurement allowing for "negative ease" and a snug, non-slouchy fit.

To ensure a very loose bind off, use a needle 1 or 2 sizes larger to bind off.

N1 and N4 hold sole sts; N2 and N3 hold instep sts.

## Socks
Using Provisional Cast On method and single dpn, cast on 30 (36) sts.

Purl 1 row.

### Short Row Toe
**Row 1 (RS):** Knit to last st, wrap and turn.

**Row 2:** Purl to last st, wrap and turn.

**Row 3:** Knit to st before last wrapped st, wrap and turn.

**Row 4:** Purl to st before last wrapped st,

wrap and turn.

Rep Rows 3 and 4 until 9 (10) sts are wrapped on each side, leaving 12 (16) sts unworked in center of row. Half of the toe is complete.

**Next row (RS):** Knit to first wrapped st, knit st tog with wrap, wrap and turn. (Next st will now have 2 wraps—on subsequent rows knit wrapped st tog with both wraps.)

**Next row:** Purl to first wrapped st, purl st tog with wrap, wrap and turn. (Next st will now have 2 wraps—on subsequent rows, knit wrapped st tog with both wraps.)

Rep last 2 rows until all sts have been worked and no wraps rem. Toe is complete.

### Foot
**Set-up rnd:** N4: k15 (18), place marker for beg of rnd; N1: k15 (18); carefully unzip the Provisional Cast On st by st and sl 15 (18) sts each to N2 and N3; pick up a running thread between N1 and N2, and with N1, knit it tbl; N2 and N3: knit; N4: pick up a running thread between N3 and N4 and knit it tbl, knit to end. (62, 74 sts)

**Rnd 1:** N1: knit to last 2 sts, k2tog; N2 and N3: work in pat; N4: ssk, knit to end. (60, 72 sts)

Continue working St st on N1 and N4 and work Undulation Pat on N2 and N3 until sock measures 7 (7¼, 7½, 8) inches or approx 1¾ inches less than desired length, ending with N3.

### Short Row Heel
Sl sts on N4 and N1 to 1 dpn for heel, keeping sts on N2 and N3 on hold.

Work short row heel as for short row toe.

### Leg
Continue in the rnd, work Undulation Pat on all sts until leg measures 6 inches or desired length.

Work in K2, P2 Rib for 1 inch.

Bind off very loosely in rib.

**Finishing**
Weave in ends, block if desired. ▼

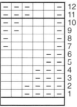

| | STITCH KEY |
|---|---|
| □ | Knit |
| − | Purl |

6-st rep
**UNDULATIONS SOCKS**

# treat for your feet

Design by Christine L. Walter

Think of the toe as the top of your sock and start knitting. That makes it easy to try on as you go for the perfect fit.

## Skill Level

■■■□ INTERMEDIATE

## Sizes

Woman's small [size 6/7] (medium [size 8/9]) Instructions are given for smaller size, with larger size in parentheses. When only 1 number is given, it applies to both sizes.

## Finished Measurements

**Circumference:** 8¼ (9¼) inches
**Foot length:** 9 (9¾) inches

## Materials

▼ Louet Gems Sport 100 percent merino wool light weight yarn (225 yds/100g per skein): 1 (2) skeins sandalwood #44 (MC) and 1 skein aqua #48 (CC)
▼ Size 2 (2.75mm) double-pointed needles (set of 5) or size needed to obtain gauge
▼ Spare needle 1–2 sizes larger
▼ Small crochet hook
▼ Stitch marker
▼ Waste yarn
▼ Tapestry needle

## Gauge

27 sts and 40 rows = 4 inches/10cm in solid-colored St st
28 sts and 33 rows = 4 inches/10cm in Two-Color Pat
To save time, take time to check gauge.

## Special Abbreviations

**Ssp:** [Sl 1 knitwise] twice, pass back to RH needle, p2tog tbl.
**Sssp:** [Sl 1 knitwise] 3 times, p3tog tbl.
**N1, N2, N3, N4:** Needles 1, 2, 3, 4.

## Pattern Stitch

**Two-Color Pat (multiple of 8 sts)**
See chart on page 143.

## Special Technique

**Provisional Cast On:** With crochet hook and waste yarn, make a chain several sts longer than desired cast on. With knitting needle and project yarn, pick up indicated number of sts in the "bumps" on back of chain. When indicated in pat, "unzip" the crochet chain to free live sts and sl to needle.

## Pattern Notes

Because feet vary in length, measure your feet and make adjustments as necessary as suggested in the pat.

Sock circumference is should be approximately 10 percent less than actual foot measurement; allowing for "negative ease" and a snug, non-slouchy fit.

On foot, N1 and N2 hold instep sts; N3 and N4 hold sole sts. On cuff, beg of rnd is at center back.

When working Two-Color Pat, be careful to carry yarn not in use very loosely on WS to ensure fabric elasticity.

To ensure a very loose bind off, use a needle 1 or 2 sizes larger to bind off.

## Sock

Using Provisional Cast On method and MC, cast on 28 (32) sts.

Knit 1 row.

## Short Row Toe

**Row 1 (RS):** Knit to last st, turn, leaving last st on needle.

**Row 2:** Wyib, yo, then purl to last st, turn, leaving last st on needle.

**Row 3:** Yo, knit to 1 st before the paired st/yo of the previous row, turn.

**Row 4:** Wyib, yo, purl to 1 st before the paired st/yo of previous row, turn.

Continue working in this manner, starting each row with a yo and ending with 1 st less than before until you have 10 (12) sts between yo's. The last turn will bring you to a RS row.

**Next row (RS):** Yo, knit to the first yo; sl yo purlwise onto the RH hand needle, then

return it to the LH needle by inserting the needle from front to back (this reverses the way the yo is mounted), k2tog, turn.

**Row 5:** Yo, purl to the first yo, ssp, turn.

**Row 6:** Yo, knit to the first yo. (There are 2 yo's side by side.) Sl both of them purlwise 1 at a time to the RH needle, then return them to the LH needle as before by inserting the needle from front to back, k3tog, turn.

**Row 7:** Yo, purl to the first yo on the next needle. Again you find 2 yo's side by side, sssp, turn.

Rep last 2 rows until all yo's of the toe have been consumed in the dec. Turn.

## Foot

**Set-up rnd:** N1: yo, k14 (16); N2: knit to last yo. Carefully unzip the Provisional Cast On st by st and sl 14 (16) sts each to N3 and N4. You should have (15, 17) sts on N1 and N2 [each needle has 1 yo plus 14 (16) sts)] and 14 (16) sts on each of N3 and N4. N3: sl the yo at the end of N2 to the beg of N3 and k2tog, k13 (15); N4: k13 (15), ssk the last st from N4 with the yo at the beg of N1; place marker for beg of rnd. (56, 64 sts; 14, 16 sts on each dpn)

**Rnd 1:** P1, [k2, p2] 6 (7) times, k2, p1, k28 (32).

Rep Rnd 1 until sock measures 7 (7¾) inches from beg or 2 inches less than desired length of foot to heel.

## Short Row Heel

Sl sts on N1 and N2 to 1 dpn for heel, sl sts on N3 and N4 to single dpn for holder.

Work short row heel as for short row toe, then continue as follows:

**Next rnd (RS):** N4: Yo, k14 (16), place marker for beg of rnd; N1: knit to last yo, transfer the yo to the dpn with sts on hold; N2: k2tog (yo and first st), k13 (15); N3: k13 (15), sl the yo from end of N4 and ssk the last st with the yo; N4: knit. (56, 64 sts)

### Cuff
Work in Two-Color Pat for 39 (42) rnds or to desired length. Do not cut yarns.

### Cuff edge
**Rnd 1:** Knit with CC.

**Rnd 2:** Purl with CC.

**Rnd 3:** *K1 MC, k1 CC; rep from * around.

**Rnd 4:** *P1 MC, k1 CC; rep from * around.

Rep Rnds 1 and 2 once more.

Bind off using 2-color bind-off method as follows: K1 CC, k1 MC, pass first st over 2nd st; continue binding off in this manner working each st in alternating color.

Cut yarn, leaving an 8-inch tail.

### Finishing
Weave in ends. Block lightly. ▼

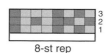

8-st rep

**TREAT FOR YOUR FEET**

COLOR KEY
■ MC
■ CC

# for
# charity

Top-down knits can

make a difference.

Here are ideas with

information on some

worthwhile charities.

# precious preemie set

Design by Nazanin S. Fard

This preemie baby jacket and hat are worked from top to bottom featuring a double seed stitch pattern.

## Skill Level
■■□□ EASY

## Finished Measurements
**Chest:** 10 inches (buttoned)
**Length:** 4½ inches
**Hat circumference:** 7 inches

## Materials
▼ Universal Bella 4 Ply 55 percent polyamide/45 percent acrylic fine weight yarn (253 yds/50g per ball): 1 ball yellow #01
▼ Size 3 (3.25mm) double-pointed and 16 or 24-inch circular needles or size needed to obtain gauge
▼ 3 small buttons
▼ Waste yarn
▼ Tapestry needle
▼ 1-inch-wide piece of cardboard for making pompom

## Gauge
34 sts and 32 rows = 4 inches/10cm in Double Seed St
To save time, take time to check gauge.

## Special Abbreviation
**M1 (Make 1):** Insert LH needle from front to back under the running thread between the last st worked and next st on LH. With RH needle, knit into the back of this lp.

## Pattern Stitch
**Double Seed St** (even number of sts)
**Rows/rnds 1 and 2:** *K1, p1; rep from * to end.
**Rows/rnds 3 and 4:** *P1, k1; rep from * to end.
Rep Rows/rnds 1–4 for pat.

## Pattern Notes
This sweater is worked from the neck down, with raglan shaping immediately preceding sleeve separation. Body is worked from underarm to bottom edge. Sleeves are worked in the rnd to cuff.

Yoke and body are worked back and forth on a circular needle.

## Jacket
### Yoke
Cast on 47 sts. Do not join.

**Rows 1 (WS)–3:** K1, *p1, k1; rep from * across.

**Row 4 (RS):** *K3, M1; rep from * to last 2 sts, k2. (62 sts)

Work 7 rows in St st, beg with a WS [purl] row.

**Next row:** K2, *M1, k1; rep from * across. (92 sts)

Work 7 rows in rev St st, beg with a WS [knit] row.

## Raglan Shaping
**Next row (RS):** K13 front sts, yo, k1, yo, k18 sleeve sts, yo, k1, yo, k26 back sts, yo, k1, yo, k18 sleeve sts, yo, k1, yo, k13 front sts. (100 sts)

**Next row:** Purl.

**Next row:** K14, yo, k1, yo, k20, yo, k1, yo, k28, yo, k1, yo, k20, yo, k1, yo, k14. (108 sts)

**Next row:** Purl.

## Separate Body & Sleeves
**Next row:** K16, cast on 6 underarm sts, sl 22 sleeve sts to waste yarn, k32, cast on 6 underarm sts, sl 22 sleeve sts to waste yarn, k16. (76 sts)

## Body
Work 28 rows in Double Seed St.

Work 6 rows in garter st.

Bind off all sts loosely.

## Sleeves
With dpns and beg at center underarm, pick up and knit 3 sts, sl sleeve sts to dpns, pick up and knit 3 sts from underarm, place marker for beg of rnd and join. (28 sts)

Work 20 rnds in Double Seed St.

Work 6 rnds of garter st [knit 1 rnd, purl 1 rnd].

Bind off loosely.

## Finishing
### Button band
With RS facing, pick up and knit 31 sts along left front.

Knit 8 rows.

Bind off.

### Buttonhole band
Beg at upper edge, pick up and knit 31 sts along right front.

Knit 3 rows.

**Buttonhole row:** K2, [yo, ssk, k3] 3 times, knit to end.

Knit 4 rows.

Bind off.

Weave in all ends. Block as necessary. Sew on buttons opposite buttonholes.

### Hat

With dpns, cast on 6 sts, distributing sts evenly on 3 needles [2 sts on each needle]; place marker for beg of rnd and join, taking care not to twist sts.

**Rnds 1, 3, 5, 7:** Knit around.

**Rnd 2:** *K1, M1; rep from * around. (12 sts)

**Rnd 4:** Rep Rnd 2. (24 sts)

**Rnd 6:** Rep Rnd 2. (48 sts)

**Rnd 8:** *K4, M1; rep from * around. (60 sts)

**Rnd 9:** Knit around.

Work even in Double Seed St until hat measures 3½ inches.

Work 8 rnds in K1, P1 Rib.

Bind off very loosely in rib.

### Finishing

Weave in all ends. Block as necessary.

### Pompom

Wrap yarn around a 1-inch piece of cardboard 30 times. Cut yarn. Insert an 8-inch strand of yarn close to the cardboard and wrap a couple of times around the wrapped yarn. Cut the other side. Secure to the top of hat. ▼

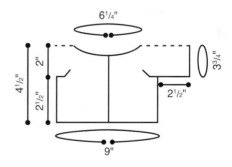

## stitches from the heart

STITCHES FROM THE HEART is a nonprofit organization that provides handmade clothing, blankets and love to premature babies all across the United States. On their Web site, www.stitchesfromtheheart.org, you can find lots of knit and crochet patterns, body measurement charts and a list of hospitals around the nation that will accept these types of garments.

To become a part of Stitches from the Heart, e-mail them at StitchFromHeart@aol.com.

# huggable hillary bear

Design by Nazanin S. Fard

Having a bear to hug and call one's own can make all the difference to a child—especially those affected by illness.

## Skill Level
◼◼◻◻ EASY

## Finished Measurement
15 inches tall

## Materials
- Red Heart Sport 100 percent acrylic light weight yarn (165 yds/70g per skein): 1 skein each fawn beige #322 (A), purple #585 (B) yellow #230 (C), and, 5 yds black #12
- Size 5 (3.75mm) double-pointed needles (set of 5) or size needed to obtain gauge
- Tapestry needle
- Waste yarn
- Fiberfill for filling the bear

## Gauge
24 sts and 32 rows = 4 inches/10cm in St st
To save time, take time to check gauge.

## Special Abbreviations
**Inc1 (Increase 1):** Knit in front and back of the next st.
**N1, N2, N3, N4:** Needles 1, 2, 3, 4, counting from beg of rnd.

## Pattern Stitch
**Garter St** (in the rnd)
Knit 1 rnd, purl 1 rnd.

## Pattern Notes
Beg of rnd is at center back.

When starting a rnd with a new-color yarn, bring up the leg of the st just made from the previous rnd and place it on the LH needle then knit it tog with first st on the needle; knit the rest of the rnd as usual.

## Bear
### Head
With A, cast on 60 sts and distribute evenly on 4 dpns (15 sts on each needle); place marker for beg of rnd and join, taking care not to twist sts.

Beg with a purl rnd, work 20 rnds in garter st.

*Next rnd: N1: Knit to last 2 sts, k2tog; N2 and N3: knit across; N4: k2tog, knit to end. (58 sts)

Continue in Garter St for 3 rnds.

**Next rnd:** N1: knit; N2: k2tog, knit to end; N3: knit to last 2 sts, k2tog; N2: knit. (56 sts)

Continue in Garter St for 3 rnds.*

Rep from * to * twice more. (48 sts, 12 on each needle)

**Next rnd:** *K2, k2tog; rep from * around. (36 sts)

**Next rnd:** Purl.

**Next rnd:** With B, knit.

### Body
**Next rnd:** Inc1 in every st around. (72 sts)

Continue in St st and knit 4 rnds B, *2 rnds C, 2 rnds B, 2 rnds C*, 6 rnds B; rep from * to *, then knit 12 rnds B.

### Divide for legs
Sl first 36 sts to waste yarn. (36 sts rem)

### Legs
Distribute sts evenly on 3 dpns (12 on each needle); place marker for beg of rnd and join.

With B, knit 12 rnds.

Change to A and work 12 rnds in Garter St, beg with a knit rnd.

**Next rnd:** *K2tog; rep from * around. (18 sts)

**Next rnd:** Purl.

**Next rnd:** K2tog around. (9 sts)

Cut yarn, leaving an 8-inch tail.

Using tapestry needle, thread tail through rem sts, and pull tight.

Sl 36 sts from waste yarn to dpns and work 2nd leg as for first.

### Arms
### Make 2
With B, cast on 30 sts and distribute on 3 dpns (10 on each needle); place marker for beg of rnd.

*Knit 6 rnds B, 2 rnds C, 2 rnds B, 2 rnds C; rep from *, then knit 6 rnds B.

Change to A and work 12 rnds in Garter St, beg with a knit rnd.

**Next rnd:** K2tog around. (15 sts)

**Next rnd:** Purl.

**Next rnd:** *K2tog, k1, k2tog; rep from * around. (9 sts)

Using tapestry needle, thread tail through rem sts, and pull tight.

Weave in all ends.

### Skirt
With B, cast on 75 sts; do not join.

**Row 1 (RS):** K1, *p1, k1; rep from * to end.

**Row 2:** P1, *k1, p1; rep from * to end.

**Row 3:** *K3, yo; rep from * to last 3 sts, k3. (99 sts)

**Rows 4, 6, 8:** Purl.

**Row 5:** *K4, yo; rep from * to last 3 sts, k3. (123 sts)

**Row 7:** *K5, yo; rep from * to last 3 sts, k3. (147 sts)

**Row 9:** *K6, yo; rep from * to last 3 sts, k3. (171 sts)

**Rows 10–13:** Knit.

Bind off all sts loosely.

### I-Cord Necktie

With C, cast on 4 sts.

*K4, do not turn, sl sts back to LH needle; rep from * until cord is measures 20 inches. Bind off.

### Finishing

Sew the skirt to the last stripe on the body.

Stuff head, body, legs and arms with fiberfill.

Sew head closed, then form ears by stitching diagonally across on both squared edges.

Sew arms to body.

Using black yarn and satin st, embroider the eyes and nose.

Using black yarn and stem st, embroider the mouth.

Tie the I-cord around the neck to make a bow. Tack in back to secure. ▼

Satin Stitch
(For Face)

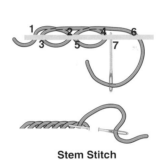

Stem Stitch

## mother bear project

The Mother Bear Project is a nonprofit organization dedicated to providing comfort and hope to children, primarily those affected by HIV/AIDS in emerging nations, by giving them a gift of love in the form of hand-knit or crocheted bears. Check out their Web site at www.motherbearproject.org

The bears are made from a World War II-era pattern which was chosen because the bears are lightweight and easy to send. Each pattern includes a tag for you to sign your first name and attach to your bear's wrist before sending it back. A red felt heart is sewn on each bear before it is shipped to a partner organization for distribution to the children. Knitters of all knitting abilities are welcome to participate. Patterns are sold for $5 only. The shipping fee for the first bear is included with the price of the pattern. Please send $3 for each additional bear you send back.

Once you have knitted your bear(s), include $3 for shipping each bear except the first and send your bears to the address below:

Mother Bear Project
P.O. Box 62188
Minneapolis, MN 55426

# easy sweaters for kids

**Blocks Pullover Design by Nazanin S. Fard**
**Striped Sweater Design by Kathy Wesley**

## These T-shaped sweaters are worked from top down and have no seams to sew.

### Skill Level
■■□□ EASY

### Blocks Pullover

### Sizes
Child's 4 (6, 8, 10) Instructions are given for smallest size, with larger sizes in parentheses. When only 1 number is given, it applies to all sizes.

### Finished Measurements
**Chest:** 27½ (29¼, 32, 34¾) inches
**Length:** 14 (15½, 17, 18½) inches

### Materials
▼ Red Heart Kids 100 percent acrylic medium weight yarn (290 yds/5 oz per skein): 2 (2, 3, 3) skeins blue #2845
▼ Size 6 (4mm) double-pointed and 24-inch circular needles
▼ Size 7 (4.5mm) 24-inch circular needle or size needed to obtain gauge
▼ Waste yarn
▼ Tapestry needle

### Gauge
18 sts and 28 rnds = 4 inches/10cm in St st with larger needle

To save time, take time to check gauge.

### Special Technique
**3-Needle Bind Off:** With RS tog and needles parallel, using a 3rd needle, knit tog a st from the front needle with 1 from the back. *Knit tog a st from the front and back needles, and sl the first st over the 2nd to bind off. Rep from * across, then fasten off last st.

### Pattern Stitch
**Blocks Pat (multiple of 5 sts + 2)**
**Rows 1 (RS)–6:** Sl 1, *k5, p5; rep from * to last st, k1.
**Rows 7–12:** Sl 1, *p5, k5; rep from * to last st, k1.
Rep Rows 1–12 for pat.

### Pattern Note
Pat is worked back and forth on a circular needle until front and back are joined, at which point it is worked in the rnd.

### Back Yoke
With smaller needle, cast on 122 (137, 152, 162) sts. Do not join.

**Rows 1–4:** Knit.

Change to larger needle and work Blocks pat for 5½ (6, 6½, 7) inches.

Sl sts to waste yarn for holder.

### Front Yoke
With RS of back facing and using smaller needle, pick up and knit 46 (53, 59, 64) sts along the right shoulder, skip center 30 (31, 34, 34) back neck sts, cast on 30 (31, 34, 34) sts for front neck, pick up and knit 46 (53, 59, 64) sts along the left shoulder. (122, 137, 152, 162 sts)

Work as for back, leaving sts on needle when finished.

### Join front & back
Sl back sts to smaller needle.

Turn WS out.

**Row 1:** Using 3-Needle Bind Off, bind off 30 (35, 40, 42) sts for underarm sleeve seam, then purl the back sts, turn.

**Row 2:** Using 3-Needle Bind Off, bind off 30 (35, 40, 42) sts for underarm sleeve seam, then purl the front sts. (124, 134, 144, 156 sts)

## Body
Turn RS out and continue with larger needle, placing marker at beg of rnd.

Work even in St st until piece measures 7½ (8½, 9½, 10½) inches or 1 inch less than desired length from underarm.

Change to smaller needle and work 8 rnds of garter st (purl 1 rnd, knit 1 rnd).

Bind off loosely.

## Finishing
### Sleeve cuffs
Using dpns, pick up and knit 1 st in every slipped st at the edge of the sleeve, place marker for beg of rnd and join.

Work 6 rnds in garter st.

Bind off loosely.

Weave in all ends. Block sweater to finished measurements.

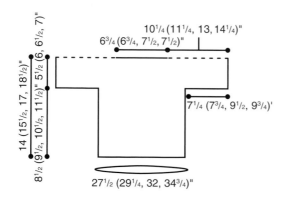

10¼ (11¼, 13, 14¼)"
6¾ (6¾, 7½, 7½)"
7¼ (7¾, 9½, 9¾)"
14 (15½, 17, 18½)"
8½ (9½, 10½, 11½)" 5½ (6, 6½, 7)"
27½ (29¼, 32, 34¾)"

# Striped Sweater

## Sizes
Child's 2 (4, 6, 8, 10) Instructions are given for smallest size, with larger sizes in parentheses. When only 1 number is given, it applies to all sizes.

## Finished Measurements
**Chest:** 26½ (28, 29½, 31¼, 32¾) inches
**Length:** 15 (16½, 18, 19½, 21) inches

## Materials
▼ Caron Simply Soft Brites 100 percent acrylic medium weight yarn (315 yds/170g per skein): 2 (2, 3, 3, 3) skeins blue mint #9608 (A), and 1 skein each limelight #9607 (B) and lemonade #9606 (C)

**4 MEDIUM**

▼ Size 7 (4.5mm) 29-inch circular knitting needles or size needed to obtain gauge
▼ Spare size 7 knitting needle
▼ Waste yarn
▼ Tapestry needle

## Gauge
20 sts and 26 rnds = 4 inches/10cm in St st
To save time, take time to check gauge.

## Special Techniques
**Provisional Cast On:** With crochet hook and waste yarn, make a chain several sts longer than desired cast on. With knitting needle and project yarn, pick up indicated number of sts in the "bumps" on back of chain. When indicated in pat, "unzip" the crochet chain and place live sts on needle.

**3-Needle Bind Off:** With RS tog and needles parallel, using a 3rd needle, knit tog a st from the front needle with 1 from the back. *Knit tog a st from the front and back needles, and sl the first st over the 2nd to bind off. Rep from * across, then fasten off last st.

## Pattern Stitch
### Stripe
*Knit 4 rnds A, knit 1 rnd B, purl 1 rnd B, knit 4 rnds A, knit 1 rnd C; rep from * for pat.

## Pattern Notes

When working provisional cast on, make 3 chains, 2 for sleeve sts, 1 for back sts.

Yoke of sweater (including sleeves) is worked back and forth from lower edge of back yoke to lower edge front yoke. Then sleeves are separated and body is worked in the rnd to bottom edge.

## Yoke & Sleeves

Using Provisional Cast On and A, cast on 28 (30, 32, 34, 36) sts for sleeve, 66 (70, 74, 78, 82) sts for back, 28 (30, 32, 34, 36) sts for sleeve. (122, 130, 138, 146, 154 total sts cast on)

With A, work across all sts in garter st until piece measures 5½ (6, 6½, 7, 7½) inches.

## Neck opening

**Next row:** K43 (47, 50, 54, 56) sts, bind off 36 (36, 38, 38, 42) sts for back neck, knit to end.

**Next row:** K43 (47, 50, 54, 56) sts, cast on

36 (36, 38, 38, 42) sts for front neck using backward lp method.

Work in garter st until piece measures 5½ (6, 6½, 7, 7½) inches from neck opening.

**Next row:** K28 (30, 32, 34, 36) sts and sl to waste yarn for sleeve; k66 (70, 74, 78, 82) sts; sl rem 28 (30, 32, 34, 36) sts to waste yarn for sleeve.

## Body
Unzip provisional cast on for 66 (70, 74, 48, 82) back sts and sl to needle; place marker for beg of rnd. (132, 140, 148, 156 164 body sts on needle)

Work Stripe pat until body measures 8 (9, 10, 11, 12) inches or 1½ inches less than desired length from underarm.

With A, work 1½ inches in K2, P2 Rib.

Bind off very loosely in rib.

## Finishing
Turn sweater WS out.

Unzip provisional cast on of back left sleeve and sl sts to needle; sl front left sleeve sts from waste yarn to 2nd needle.

Using spare needle, work 3-Needle Bind Off to join underarm seam.

Rep for right sleeve.

Weave in loose ends. Block to finished measurements. ▼

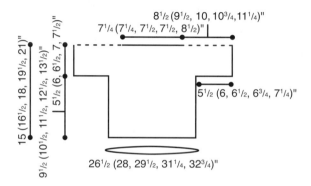

# wooly pulley
# helmet liner

Design by Nazanin S. Fard

This easy helmet liner is worked from the top in stockinette stitch, 2 x 2 ribbing and garter stitch.

**Skill Level**

 ◼◼◻◻ EASY

**Size**
Man's average

**Finished Measurements**
**Circumference of top:** 21½ inches
**Length:** 13½ inches

**Materials**
▼ Moda Dea Washable Wool 100 percent merino wool superwash medium weight yarn (166 yds/100g per ball): 2 balls moss #4440
▼ Size 6 (4mm) double-pointed and 16-inch circular needles
▼ Size 8 (5mm) double-pointed and 16-inch circular needles or size needed to obtain gauge
▼ Medium-size crochet hook
▼ Waste yarn
▼ Tapestry needle

**Gauge**
20 sts and 26 rnds = 4 inches/10cm in St st with larger needles
To save time, take time to check gauge.

## Special Abbreviation

**M1 (Make 1):** Insert LH needle from front to back under the running thread between the last sth worked and next st on LH. With RH needle, knit into the back of this lp.

## Special Techniques

**Emily Ocker's Cast On:** See illustrations on this page.
**Provisional Cast On:** With crochet hook and waste yarn, make a chain several sts longer than desired cast on. With knitting needle and project yarn, pick up indicated number of sts in the "bumps" on back of chain. When indicated in pat, "unzip" the crochet chain to free live sts.

## Pattern Note

Change from dpns to circular needle when it is comfortable to do so.

## Instructions

With larger dpns and using Emily Ocker's cast-on method, cast on 9 sts. Distribute evenly on 3 dpns (3 on each); place marker for beg of rnd and join, taking care not to twist sts.

**Rnd 1:** Knit.

### Emily Ocker's circular cast on:
Make a slip knot.

**1.** Wrap yarn around crochet hook and pull through slip knot.

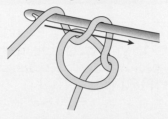

**2.** Wrap yarn around hook and pull through loop on hook.

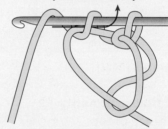

**3.** Repeat steps 1 and 2 as many times necessary.

**4.** When you have as many stitches as you like, pull short end of slip knot to make it round and distribute stitches on knitting needle.

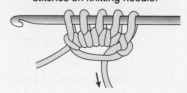

**Rnd 2:** *K1, M1; rep from * around. (18 sts)

**Rnds 3, 5, 7, 9:** Knit.

**Rnd 4:** Rep Rnd 2. (36 sts)

**Rnd 6:** *K2, M1; rep from * around. (54 sts)

**Rnd 8:** Rep Rnd 6. (81 sts)

**Rnd 10:** *K3, M1; rep from * around. (108 sts)

Work even in St st for 5 inches.

**Next rnd:** With smaller needle, k50, leaving the rem 58 sts on larger needle for the forehead part of helmet liner, then provisionally cast on 50 sts, place marker and join with the rest of sts on needle. (100 sts)

Work K2, P2 Rib for 7½ inches.

Bind off loosely in rib.

### Finishing
Unzip the Provisional Cast On and sl 50 sts and 58 sts on larger needle to smaller circular needle, place marker for beg of rnd and join. (108 sts)

**Rnd 1:** *K7, k2tog; rep from * around. (96 sts)

**Rnds 2–4:** Work in garter st (purl 1 rnd, knit 1 rnd).

**Rnd 5:** *K6, k2tog; rep from * around. (84 sts)

**Rnds 6–8:** Continue in garter st.

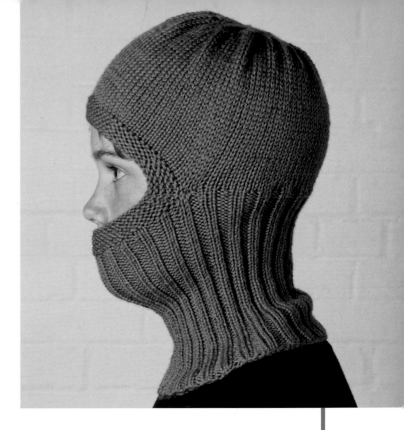

**Rnd 9:** *K5, k2tog; rep from * around. (72 sts)

**Rnd 10:** Purl around.

Bind off all sts.

Weave in all ends. Block as necessary. ▼

## operation helmet liner

During any war, civilians have had a major role in supporting the armed forces. In World War I and World War II, volunteers provided handmade wool gloves, socks and stocking caps for the soldiers during wintertime. Now, our armed forces deployed during the winter months, especially those in the mountains of Afghanistan and the deserts of Iraq, as well as Kosovo and South Korea, need our help to keep warm. Unlike synthetic fibers, the 100 percent wool helmet liners, known by our armed forces as "Wooly Pulleys," that knitters make are inherently nonflammable. This means that in the event of a fire, the wool fibers do not melt against the skin causing worse injuries. In addition, wool is warmer than synthetic fibers even when wet.

Besides warming our armed forces physically, the wool helmet liners warm their hearts. One soldier called the helmet liners, "genuine, home-issued gear" and was especially grateful for something handmade from home.

You can use this pattern or go to: www.geocities.com/helmetliner for more patterns.

Send finished helmet liners to:

Operation Helmet Liner
P.O. Box 236
Auburn, IL 62615

# comfy chemo caps

Designs by Nazanin S. Fard

Use soft yarns that won't irritate sensitive skin for two knit styles that will be a little more comfy.

**Skill Level**

 EASY

**Size**
Woman's average

### Cable Ribbed Cap
**Finished Measurement**
**Circumference:** 20½ inches

**Materials**
▼ Moda Dea Fashionista 50 percent acrylic /50 percent Tencel/Lyocell medium weight yarn (183 yds/100g per ball): 1 ball blue jean #6130
▼ Size 8 (5mm) double-pointed (set of 5) and 16-inch circular needle or size needed to obtain gauge
▼ Tapestry needle

**Gauge**
19 sts and 26 rnds = 4 inches/10cm in Cabled Rib
To save time, take time to check gauge.

**Special Abbreviations**
**Inc1 (Increase 1):** Knit in front and back of st.
**LC (Left Cross):** With RH needle behind LH needle, skip 1 st and knit the 2nd st through

the back lp; insert RH needle into the backs of both sts (the skipped st and the 2nd st) and k2tog-tbl.

## Pattern Stitch
**Cabled Rib** (multiple of 4 sts)
**Rnd 1:** *K2, p2; rep from * around.
**Rnd 2:** *LC, p2; rep from * around.
Rep Rnds 1 and 2 for pat.

## Pattern Note
Change to circular needle when sts will fit comfortably on it.

## Cap
With dpn, cast on 4 sts; distribute sts to 4 dpns; place marker for beg of rnd, join taking care not to twist sts.

**Rnd 1:** Knit.

**Rnds 2, 4, 6, 8:** Inc1 in every st. (64 sts)

**Rnds 3, 5, 7, 9:** Purl.

**Rnd 10:** *Inc1, k1; rep from * around. (96 sts)

Work in Cabled Rib until piece measures 8 inches from top.

Work K2, P2 Rib for 2 inches.

Bind off very loosely in rib.

## I-cord decoration
Leaving an 8-inch tail, cast on 3 sts.

*K3, do not turn, sl sts back to LH needle; rep from * until cord measures 40 inches.

Bind off, leaving an 8-inch tail.

Wrap the cord around 2 fingers. Pass the tails through the lps to create a pompom shape. Attach and secure to top of hat.

Weave in all ends.

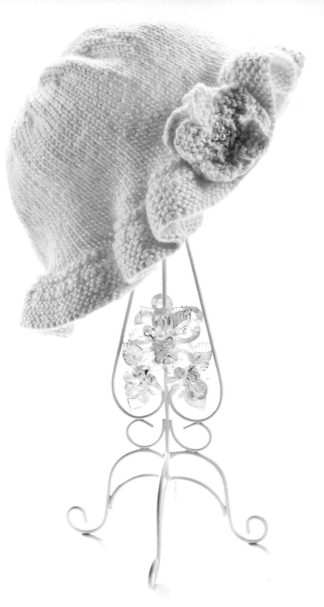

## Cap with Brim
### Finished Measurement
**Circumference (before brim):** 21½ inches

### Materials
▼ Lion Brand Lion Cashmere Blend 72 percent merino wool, 15 percent nylon, 13 percent cashmere medium weight yarn (84 yds/40g per ball): 3 balls light blue #105
▼ Size 8 (5mm) double-pointed and 16-inch circular needles or size needed to obtain gauge
▼ Sewing needle and matching thread
▼ 6 (4mm) pearls (optional)
▼ Tapestry needle

### Gauge
18 sts and 26 rnds = 4 inches/10cm in St st
To save time, take time to check gauge.

### Special Abbreviations
**Inc1 (Increase 1):** Knit in front and back of st.
**M1 (Make 1):** Insert LH needle from front to back under the running thread between the last st worked and next st on LH needle. With RH needle, knit into the back of this lp.

### Pattern Stitch
**Garter St** (in the rnd)
**Rnd 1:** Purl.
**Rnd 2:** Knit.
Rep Rnds 1 and 2 for pat.

### Cap
With dpn, cast on 3 sts; distribute to 3 dpns; place marker for beg of rnd and join, taking care not to twist sts.

**Rnd 1:** Inc1 around. (6 sts)

**Rnd 2 and all even-numbered rnds:** Knit.

**Rnd 3:** *K1, M1; rep from * around. (12 sts)

**Rnd 5:** Rep Rnd 3. (24 sts)

**Rnd 7:** *K2, M1; rep from * around. (36 sts)

**Rnd 9:** *K3, M1; rep from * around. (48 sts)

**Rnd 11:** *K4, M1; rep from * around. (60 sts)

**Rnd 13:** *K5, M1; rep from * around. (72 sts)

**Rnd 15:** *K6, M1; rep from * around. (84 sts)

**Rnd 17:** *K7, M1; rep from * around. (96 sts)

Work even in St st for 4 inches.

### Brim
**Rnd 1:** *Inc1, k1; rep from * around. (144 sts)

**Rnds 2–4:** Work in Garter St, beg with a purl rnd.

**Rnd 5:** Rep Rnd 1. (216 sts)

**Rnds 6–14:** Work in Garter St.

Bind off all sts loosely.

### Finishing
Weave in all ends. Block as necessary.

### Flower
**Lower row petals**
Cast on 5 sts.

**Rows 1–4:** Inc1, knit to end. (9 sts)

**Row 5:** Knit. Cut yarn leaving a 6-inch tail, but leave sts on needle.

Knit 4 more petals the same way. Do not cut yarn for the last petal.

### Join petals
**Row 1:** Knit across all 5 petals. (45 sts)

**Row 2:** K2tog across to last st, k1. (23 sts)

**Row 3:** K2tog across to last st, k1. (12 sts)

**Row 4:** K2tog across. (6 sts)

Cut yarn leaving an 8-inch tail.

Weave in all ends.

**Upper row petals**
Cast on 3 sts.

**Rows 1–4:** Inc1, knit to end. (7 sts)

**Row 5:** Knit. Cut yarn leaving a 6-inch tail, but leave sts on needle.

Knit 4 more petals the same way. Do not cut yarn for the last petal.

**Join petals**
**Row 1:** Knit across all 5 petals. (35 sts)

**Row 2:** K2tog across to last st, k1. (18 sts)

**Row 3:** K2tog across. (9 sts)

**Row 4:** K2tog across to last st, k1. (5 sts)

Cut yarn leaving an 8-inch tail. Using tapestry needle, thread tail through rem sts, and pull tight, then secure tail.

Weave in all ends.

Place the upper row petals on the center of the lower petals and sew the center tog.

Sew the flower on the side of the hat, right above the brim.

With sewing needle and matching thread, sew the pearls to the center of flower for decoration. ▼

# chemocaps

Ronni Lynn Spoll created www.chemocaps.com to perpetuate her daughter Heather's memory after she passed away from a rare form of cancer.  Heather was a highly regarded artist as well as a passionate knitter.

The Heather Spoll "No Hair Day" Hat Program is comprised of individual knitters and groups of knitters all over the United States and the world who knit up chemocaps and donate them to hospitals, hospices and cancer-treatment centers in their community or closest to where they live. The concept is "neighbors helping neighbors." Each chemocap has a little tag attached to it which reads the following:

Heather Spoll "No Hair Day" Hat Program
Hand-Knit by (individual's or group's name)
(and/or)
Hand-Knit in Honor of (name)
Each cancer patient who receives a hand-knit chemocap from this program knows that there is someone out there who cares for their comfort and well-being.

Most cancer patients wear very soft chemocaps to sleep in because no matter how gently linens are washed, pillowcases can be a bit scratchy and irritating to a sensitive scalp made bare because of loss of hair due to cancer treatments. Also, sleeping in a hand-knit chemocap helps retain body warmth.

For more information check out, www.chemocaps.com

## saddle-shoulder tunic
continued from 21

rem along shoulder]; pick up and knit 40 (44, 48, 48) sts to underarm, place marker for beg of rnd and join. (99, 107, 115, 115 sts)

**Rnds 1 and 2:** K2, [p1, k3] 1 (2, 3, 3) times, *[p1, k3] twice, p1, k4; rep from * 5 more times, [p1, k3] 3 (4, 5, 5) times, p1, k2.

**Rnd 3:** K2, [p1, k3] 1 (2, 3, 3) times, *[p1, k3] twice, p1, C4F; rep from * twice more; **[p1, k3] twice, p1, C4B; rep from ** twice more; [p1, k3] 3 (4, 5, 5) times, p1, k2.

**Rnd 4:** Rep Rnd 1.

Rep Rnds 1–4 for pat and work even for 4 rnds.

**Dec rnd:** K2, p1, ssk, work in pat as established to last 5 sts, k2tog, p1, k2. (97, 105, 113, 113 sts)

Rep Dec rnd [every 8th rnd] twice more, then [every 4th rnd] 17 (19, 21, 21) times. (59, 63, 67, 67 sts)

Work even until sleeve measures 16 (17, 18, 18½) inches or 2 inches less than desired length.

**Next rnd:** Dec 23 sts evenly spaced around. (36, 40, 44, 44 sts)

Change to smaller dpns and work K1, P1 rib for 2 inches.

Bind off loosely in rib.

**Right Sleeve**
Work as for Left Sleeve.

**Finishing**
**Neck**
With RS facing, using smaller 16-inch circular needle and beg at bottom right of neck opening, pick up and knit 44 (48, 52, 52) sts along front neck; 17 sts from shoulder; 49 (39, 39, 39) sts along back edge; 17 sts from shoulder; 44 (48, 52, 52) sts from left side. Do not join. (179, 169, 177, 177 sts)

**Row 1 (WS):** P2, *k1, p1; rep from * to last st, p1.

**Row 2 (RS):** K2, *p1, k1; rep from * to last st, k1.

Rep [Rows 1 and 2] 3 times.

Bind off loosely in rib.

Sew edges of neck rib to front neck cast on, overlapping them.

Weave in all ends. Block to finished measurements. ▼

---

## winter sky cardigan
continued from 25

**Button Band**
With RS facing, pick up and knit 110 (115, 119, 123, 129) sts along left front edge, including neckband.

Knit 8 rows.

Bind off.

**Buttonhole Band**
Place 6 evenly spaced markers along right front for buttonholes.

With RS facing, pick up and knit 110 (115, 119, 123, 129) sts along right front edge, including neckband.

Knit 3 rows.

**Buttonhole row:** Knit across, making buttonholes opposite markers by binding off 2 sts.

**Next row:** Knit across, casting on 2 sts above bound-off sts.

Knit 3 rows.

Bind off.

### Finishing
Weave in all ends. Block to finished measurements.

Sew buttons on button band opposite buttonholes. ▼

---

## warm woven jacket
**continued from 64**

for underarm, sl back sts to LH needle and work in pat across, cast on 8 (8, 18, 18, 28) sts for underarm, work in pat across right front.

**Next row:** Work across, working side edge and underarm sts in pat as established.

Continue in pat until neck shaping is complete. (182, 202, 222, 242, 262 sts)

Work even until piece measures approx 16½ (16½, 15½, 15½, 15½ ) inches from underarm or 1½ inches short of desired length, ending with a WS row.

### Ribbing
Change to smaller needle.

**Row 1 (RS):** K1, *k2, p2; rep from * to last st, k1.

**Row 2:** P1, *p2, k2; rep from * to last st, p1.

**Rows 3–10:** Rep [Rows 1 and 2] 4 times.

Bind off all sts loosely in pat.

### Sleeves
With RS facing and using larger needle, pick up and knit 82 (82, 102, 102, 102) sts along

front and back armhole, leaving underarm sts untouched.

Work even in Woven St pat for 7 (7, 13, 13, 21) rows.

**Dec row (RS):** K1, ssk, work in pat to last 3 sts, k2tog, k1. (80, 80, 100, 100, 100)

Rep Dec row [every 6th row] 13 (11, 11, 9, 9) times then [every 4th row] 0 (2, 2, 4, 4) time(s). (54, 54, 74, 74, 74 sts)

Work even until sleeve measures 17½ inches or 2½ inches short of desired length, ending with a WS row.

**Cuff**
Change to smaller needle.

**Row 1 (RS):** K1, *k2, p2; rep from * to last st, k1.

**Row 2:** P1, *p2, k2; rep from * to last st, p1.

Rep [Rows 1 and 2] 9 times.

Bind off all sts loosely in pat.

**Finishing**
**Front band**
On right front, place 7 markers evenly spaced between bottom of V-neck and lower edge.

With RS facing and using smaller needle, pick up and knit 100 sts along the right front; k28 (30, 30, 34, 34) back neck sts from holder, pick up and knit 100 sts along the left front edge. (228, 230, 230, 234, 234 sts)

**Rows 1–4:** Knit.

**Row 5 (buttonhole row):** Knit, working 1-Row Buttonhole opposite each marker.

**Row 6:** Knit, working (k1, k1-tbl) in double-yo buttonholes.

**Rows 7 and 8:** Knit.

Bind off all sts loosely. Sew sleeve and underarm seams. Block jacket to finished measurements.

Sew on buttons opposite buttonholes. ▼

---

## school days cardi
**continued from 71**

neck edge, and 8 (8, 9, 10, 11) sts along left front neck. (40, 40, 44, 48, 52 sts)

Work 4 rows in rev St st.

Bind off very loosely.

**Button band**
With RS facing, pick up and knit 45 (49, 61, 67, 75) st along left front edge.

Work 4 rows in rev St st.

Bind off knitwise on WS.

**Buttonhole band**
Place 4 (4, 5, 5, 5) markers evenly spaced along right front.

With RS facing, pick up and knit 45 (49, 61, 67, 75) sts along right front edge.

Knit 1 row, purl 1 row.

**Next row (WS):** Knit, working buttonholes opposite markers.

Purl 1 row.

Bind off knitwise on WS.

Weave in all ends. Block to finished measurements. Sew on buttons opposite buttonholes. ▼

## natural beauty for baby

**continued from 105**

**Rnd 2 and all even-numbered rnds:** Knit.

**Rnd 3:** *K1, yo, k1; rep from * around. (9 sts)

**Rnd 5:** *[K1, yo] twice, k1; rep from * around. (15 sts)

**Rnd 7:** *K1, yo, k3, yo, k1; rep from * around. (21 sts)

**Rnd 9:** *K1, yo, k5, yo, k1; rep from * around. (27 sts)

**Rnd 11:** *Yo, k1, yo, ssk, k3, k2tog, yo, k1; rep from * around. (30 sts)

**Rnd 13:** *K1, yo, k2, yo, ssk, k1, k2tog, yo, k2, yo; rep from * around. (36 sts)

**Rnd 15:** *K2, yo, k3, yo, sk2p, yo, k3, yo, k1; rep from * around. (42 sts)

**Rnd 17:** *K3, yo, k9, yo, k2; rep from * around. (48 sts)

**Rnd 19:** *K4, yo, k9, yo, k3; rep from * around. (54 sts)

**Rnd 21:** *K5, yo, k9, yo, k4; rep from * around. (60 sts)

Purl 2 rnds.

[Rep Rnds 1–16 of Lace pat] twice.

[Knit 1 rnd, purl 1 rnd] 3 times.

Bind off all sts loosely.

Block. ▼

---

## ahoy little mate

**continued from 117**

maintaining 4 sts on each side in garter st for front border, work in St st until piece measures 5¼ (5½, 6) inches, ending with a WS row.

**Shape back**
**Row 1 (RS):** K28 (30, 32), k2tog, k1, k2tog, k28, (30, 32). (59, 63, 67 sts)

**Rows 2, 4, 6:** K4, purl to last 4 sts, k4.

**Row 3:** K27 (29, 31), k2tog, k1, k2tog, k27 (29, 31). (57, 61, 65 sts)

**Row 5:** K26 (28, 30), k2tog, k1, k2tog, k26 (28, 30). (55, 59, 63 sts)

Cut yarn and sl first 28 (30, 32) sts to first dpn, then sl rem 27 (29, 31) sts to 2nd dpn.

With WS facing, fold in half so needles are parallel; reattach yarn at folded edge.

**Bind-off row:** K1 from first dpn (center st), then work 3-Needle Bind Off across all rem sts.

**Ties**
**Make 2**
With larger needle and MC, cast on 48 sts.

Bind off all sts, leaving 12-inch tail.

Using tail, attach end of tie securely to bottom front edge.

Weave in all ends. Block to finished measurements. ▼

# knitting stitch guide & general information

## Cast On

Leaving an end about an inch long for each stitch to be cast on, make a slip knot on the right needle.

Place the thumb and index finger of your left hand between the yarn ends with the long yarn end over your thumb, and the strand from the skein over your index finger. Close your other fingers over the strands to hold them against your palm. Spread your thumb and index fingers apart and draw the yarn into a "V."

Place the needle in front of the strand around your thumb and bring it underneath this strand. Carry the needle over and under the strand on your index finger.

Draw through loop on thumb.

Drop the loop from your thumb and draw up the strand to form a stitch on the needle.

Repeat until you have cast on the number of stitches indicated in the pattern. Remember to count the beginning slip knot as a stitch.

## Cable Cast On

This type of cast on is used when adding stitches in the middle or at the end of a row.

Make a slip knot on the left needle. Knit a stitch in this knot and place it on the left needle. Insert the right needle between the last two stitches on the left needle. Knit a stitch and place it on the left needle. Repeat for each stitch needed.

## Knit (k)

Insert tip of right needle from front to back in next stitch on left needle. Bring yarn under and over the tip of the right needle.

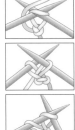

Pull yarn loop through the stitch with right needle point.

Slide the stitch off the left needle. The new stitch is on the right needle.

## Purl (p)

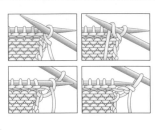

With yarn in front, insert tip of right needle from back to front through next stitch on the left needle. Bring yarn around the right needle counterclockwise.

With right needle, draw yarn back through the stitch.

Slide the stitch off the left needle. The new stitch is on the right needle.

## Bind Off

### Binding off (knit)

Knit first two stitches on left needle. Insert tip of left needle into first stitch worked on right needle and pull it over the second stitch and completely off the needle.

Knit the next stitch and repeat. When one stitch remains on right needle, cut yarn and draw tail through last stitch to fasten off.

### Binding off (purl)

Purl first two stitches on left needle. Insert tip of left needle into first stitch worked on right needle and pull it over the second stitch and completely off the needle.

Purl the next stitch and repeat. When one stitch remains on right needle, cut yarn and draw tail through last stitch to fasten off.

## Increase (inc)
## Two stitches in one stitch

### Increase (knit)

Knit the next stitch in the usual manner, but don't remove the stitch from the left needle. Place right needle behind left needle and knit again into the back of the same stitch. Slip original stitch off left needle.

### Increase (purl)

Purl the next stitch in the usual manner, but don't remove the stitch from the left needle. Place right needle behind left needle and purl again into the back of the same stitch. Slip original stitch off left needle.

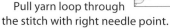

## Invisible Increase (M1)

There are several ways to make or increase one stitch.

### Make 1 with Left Twist (M1L)

Insert left needle from front to back under the horizontal loop between the last stitch worked and next stitch on left needle.

With right needle, knit into the back of this loop.

To make this increase on the purl side, insert left needle in same manner and purl into the back of the loop.

### Make 1 with Right Twist (M1R)

Insert left needle from back to front under the horizontal loop between the last stitch worked and next stitch on left needle.

With right needle, knit into the front of this loop.

To make this increase on the purl side, insert left needle in same manner and purl into the front of the loop.

### Make 1 with Backward Loop over the right needle

With your thumb, make a loop over the right needle.

Slip the loop from your thumb onto the needle and pull to tighten.

### Make 1 in top of stitch below

Insert tip of right needle into the stitch on left needle one row below.

Knit this stitch, then knit the stitch on the left needle.

## Decrease (dec)

### Knit 2 together (k2tog)

Put tip of right needle through next two stitches on left needle as to knit. Knit these two stitches as one.

### Purl 2 together (p2tog)

Put tip of right needle through next two stitches on left needle as to purl. Purl these two stitches as one.

### Slip, Slip, Knit (ssk)

Slip next two stitches, one at a time, as to knit from left needle to right needle.

Insert left needle in front of both stitches and work off needle together.

### Slip, Slip, Purl (ssp)

Slip next two stitches, one at a time, as to knit from left needle to right needle. Slip these stitches back onto left needle keeping them twisted.

Purl these two stitches together through back loops.

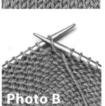

## Working Short Rows

### Wrap/Turn (w/t)
### Work as follows:

*Work to indicated turning point, take yarn to right side of fabric (in front on knit row, in back on purl row), slip next stitch purlwise, take yarn to wrong side of fabric (Photo A).

Turn work. Slip stitch, purlwise to right needle (Photo B).

Repeat from * until short rows are completed.

When all wraps are completed, work across row using the following method to work wrap and stitch together.

On knit side, insert tip of right needle into wrap, then into stitch and knit them together (Photo C).

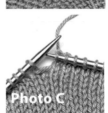

On purl side, insert tip of right needle into wrap from right side, lift it onto left needle, then purl stitch and wrap together.

---

### 3-Needle Bind Off

Use this technique for seaming two edges together, such as when joining a shoulder seam. Hold the edge stitches on two separate needles with right sides together.

With a third needle, knit together a stitch from the front needle with one from the back.

Repeat, knitting a stitch from the front needle with one from the back needle once more.

Slip the first stitch over the second.

Repeat knitting, a front and back pair of stitches together, then bind one off.

## Mattress Seam

This type of seam may be used for vertical seams (like sleave seams). It is worked with the right sides of the pieces facing you, making it easier to match stitches for stripe patterns. It is worked between the first and second stitch at the edge of the piece and works best when the first stitch is a selvage stitch.

To work this seam, thread a tapestry needle with matching yarn. Insert the needle into one corner of work from back to front, just above the cast-on stitch, leaving a 3-inch tail. Take needle to edge of other piece and bring it from back to front at the corner of this piece.

Return to the first piece and insert the needle from the right to wrong side where the thread comes out of the piece. Slip the needle upward under two horizontal threads and bring the needle through to the right side.

Cross to the other side and repeat the same process, going down where you came out, under two threads and up.

Continue working back and forth on the two pieces in the same manner for about an inch, then gently pull on the thread pulling the two pieces together (Photo A).

Complete the seam and fasten off.
Use the beginning tail to even up the lower edge by working a figure 8 between the cast-on stitches at the corners. Insert the threaded needle from front to back under both threads of the corner cast-on stitch on the edge opposite the tail, and then into the same stitch on the first edge. Pull gently until the "8" fills the gap (Photo B).

When a project is made with a textured yarn that will not pull easily through the pieces, it is recommended that a smooth yarn of the same color be used to work the seam.

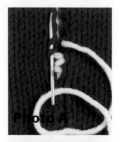

**Photo B**

### A Word About Gauge

A correct stitch gauge is very important. Please take the time to work a stitch-gauge swatch about 4 x 4 inches. Measure the swatch. If the number of stitches and rows are fewer than indicated under "Gauge" in the pattern, your needles are too large. Try another swatch with smaller needles. If the number of stitches and rows are more than indicated under "Gauge" in the pattern, your needles are too small. Try another swatch with larger needles.

## INCHES INTO MILLIMETERS & CENTIMETERS (Rounded off slightly)

| inches | mm | cm | inches | cm | inches | cm | inches | cm |
|---|---|---|---|---|---|---|---|---|
| 1/8 | 3 | 0.3 | 5 | 12.5 | 21 | 53.5 | 38 | 96.5 |
| 1/4 | 6 | 0.6 | 5 1/2 | 14 | 22 | 56 | 39 | 99 |
| 3/8 | 10 | 1 | 6 | 15 | 23 | 58.5 | 40 | 101.5 |
| 1/2 | 13 | 1.3 | 7 | 18 | 24 | 61 | 41 | 104 |
| 5/8 | 15 | 1.5 | 8 | 20.5 | 25 | 63.5 | 42 | 106.5 |
| 3/4 | 20 | 2 | 9 | 23 | 26 | 66 | 43 | 109 |
| 7/8 | 22 | 2.2 | 10 | 25.5 | 27 | 68.5 | 44 | 112 |
| 1 | 25 | 2.5 | 11 | 28 | 28 | 71 | 45 | 114.5 |
| 1 1/4 | 32 | 3.2 | 12 | 30.5 | 29 | 73.5 | 46 | 117 |
| 1 1/2 | 38 | 3.8 | 13 | 33 | 30 | 76 | 47 | 119.5 |
| 1 3/4 | 45 | 4.5 | 14 | 35.5 | 31 | 79 | 48 | 122 |
| 2 | 50 | 5 | 15 | 38 | 32 | 81.5 | 49 | 124.5 |
| 2 1/2 | 65 | 6.5 | 16 | 40.5 | 33 | 84 | 50 | 127 |
| 3 | 75 | 7.5 | 17 | 43 | 34 | 86.5 | | |
| 3 1/2 | 90 | 9 | 18 | 46 | 35 | 89 | | |
| 4 | 100 | 10 | 19 | 48.5 | 36 | 91.5 | | |
| 4 1/2 | 115 | 11.5 | 20 | 51 | 37 | 94 | | |

## KNITTING NEEDLES CONVERSION CHART

| U.S. | 0 | 1 | 2 | 3 | 4 | 5 | 6 | 7 | 8 | 9 | 10 | 10 1/2 | 11 | 13 | 15 |
|---|---|---|---|---|---|---|---|---|---|---|---|---|---|---|---|
| Metric(mm) | 2 | 2 1/4 | 2 3/4 | 3 1/4 | 3 1/2 | 3 3/4 | 4 | 4 1/2 | 5 | 5 1/2 | 6 | 6 1/2 | 8 | 9 | 10 |

## Standard Abbreviations

[ ] work instructions within brackets as many times as directed

( ) work instructions within parentheses in the place directed

** repeat instructions following the asterisks as directed

* repeat instructions following the single asterisk as directed

" inch(es)

**approx** approximately

**beg** begin/beginning

**CC** contrasting color

**ch** chain stitch

**cm** centimeter(s)

**cn** cable needle

**dec** decrease/decreases/decreasing

**dpn(s)** double-pointed needle(s)

**g** gram(s)

**inc** increase/increases/increasing

**k** knit

**k2tog** knit 2 stitches together

**LH** left hand

**lp(s)** loop(s)

**m** meter(s)

**M1** make 1 stitch

**MC** main color

**mm** millimeter(s)

**oz** ounce(s)

**p** purl

**pat(s)** pattern(s)

**p2tog** purl 2 stitches together

**psso** pass slipped stitch over

**p2sso** pass 2 slipped stitches over

**rem** remain/remaining

**rep(s)** repeat(s)

**rev St st** reverse Stockinette stitch

**RH** right hand

**rnd(s)** round(s)

**RS** right side

**skp** slip, knit, pass stitch over—1 stitch decreased

**sk2p** slip 1, knit 2 together, pass slip stitch over the knit 2 together—2 stitches decreased

**sl** slip

**sl 1k** slip 1 knitwise

**sl 1p** slip 1 purlwise

**sl st(s)** slip stitch(es)

**ssk** slip, slip, knit these 2 stitches together—a decrease

**ssp** slip next 2 stitches as to knit, slip back to left needle and purl together through back loops—a decrease

**st(s)** stitch(es)

**St st** stockinette stitch/stocking stitch

**tbl** through back loop(s)

**tog** together

**WS** wrong side

**wyib** with yarn in back

**wyif** with yarn in front

**yd(s)** yard(s)

**yfwd** yarn forward

**yo** yarn over

## Glossary

**bind off**—used to finish an edge.

**cast on**—process of making foundation stitches used in knitting.

**decrease**—means of reducing the number of stitches in a row.

**increase**—means of adding to the number of stitches in a row.

**intarsia**—method of knitting a multicolored pattern into the fabric.

**knitwise**—insert needle into stitch as if to knit.

**make 1**—method of increasing using the strand between the last stitch worked and the next stitch.

**place marker**—placing a purchased marker or loop of contrasting yarn onto the needle for ease in working a pattern repeat or into the fabric to mark a given position.

**purlwise**—insert needle into stitch as if to purl.

**right side**—side of garment or piece that will be seen when worn.

**selvage stitch**—edge stitch used to make seaming easier.

**slip, slip, knit**—a left-leaning decrease which mirrors the right-leaning "knit 2 together" decrease.

**slip stitch**—an unworked stitch slipped from left needle to right needle, usually as if to purl.

**wrong side**—side that will be inside when garment is worn.

**work even**—continue to work in the pattern as established without working any increases or decreases.

**work in pattern as established**—continue to work following the pattern stitch as it has been set up or established on the needle, working any increases or decreases in such a way that the established pattern remains the same.

**yarn over**—method of increasing by wrapping the yarn over the right needle without working a stitch.

## Skill Levels

■□□□ 
**BEGINNER**

Beginner projects using basic stitches. Minimal shaping.

■■□□ 
**EASY**

Easy projects using basic stitches, repetitive stitch patterns, simple color changes and simple shaping and finishing.

■■■□ 
**INTERMEDIATE**

Intermediate projects with a variety of stitches, mid-level shaping and finishing.

■■■■ 
**EXPERIENCED**

Experienced projects using advanced techniques and stitches, detailed shaping and refined finishing.

## Standard Yarn Weight System

Categories of yarn, gauge ranges, and recommended needle sizes

| Yarn Weight Symbol & Category Names | 1 SUPER FINE | 2 FINE | 3 LIGHT | 4 MEDIUM | 5 BULKY | 6 SUPER BULKY |
|---|---|---|---|---|---|---|
| Type of Yarns in Category | Sock, Fingering, Baby | Sport, Baby | DK, Light Worsted | Worsted, Afghan, Aran | Chunky, Craft, Rug | Bulky, Roving |
| Knit Gauge* Ranges in Stockinette Stitch to 4 inches | 21–32 sts | 23–26 sts | 21–24 sts | 16–20 sts | 12–15 sts | 6–11 sts |
| Recommended Needle in Metric Size Range | 2.25–3.25mm | 3.25–3.75mm | 3.75–4.5mm | 4.5–5.5mm | 5.5–8mm | 8mm |
| Recommended Needle U.S. Size Range | 1 to 3 | 3 to 5 | 5 to 7 | 7 to 9 | 9 to 11 | 11 and larger |

* GUIDELINES ONLY: The above reflect the most commonly used gauges and needle sizes for specific yarn categories.

# photo index

# special thanks

## We would like to thank the talented knitting designers whose work is featured in this collection.

**Phoenix Bess**
Making News Cap, 124

**Nazanin S. Fard**
Blocks Pullover, 154
Cellular T-Top, 42
Comfy Chemo Caps, 162
Huggable Hillary Bear, 151
Natural Beauty for Baby, 102
Precious Preemie Set, 146
Warm Woven Jacket, 63
Wooly Pulley Helmet Liner, 159

**Cecily Glowik**
Quick Unisex Hats, 131
Toasty Friend, 94

**Sara Louise Harper**
Ruby Layer, 76
Shades for Play, 73

**Andra Knight-Bowman**
Cable & Rib Comfort, 58

**Carol May**
Saddle-Shoulder Tunic, 19

**Joyce Nordstrom**
Ahoy Little Mate!, 115
Allover Cabling, 14
Busy Day Dress, 111
Give Him a Vee, 84
Joy-to-Wear Cardi, 27
Soothing Waves, 35

**Debbie O'Neill**
Classic Unisex Cardigan, 118
Oh Baby Chevron, 30

**Celeste Pinheiro**
Gentle Lace, 46
Harmony Kimono, 38

**Amy Polcyn**
Summer Breeze Top, 51
Undulations Socks, 137

**Susan Robicheau**
Awesome Cables, 53
School Days Cardi, 69
Styled for Fun, 80
Winter Sky Cardigan, 22

**Kathy Sasser**
The Warm Button Set, 129

**Pauline Schultz**
Baby Goes Visiting, 107
Rugged Ribbed Sweater, 89

**Christine L. Walter**
Bavarian Style, 134
Treat for Your Feet, 140

**Kathy Wesley**
Down & Doggie, 97
Striped Sweater, 154

# buyer's guide

**Berroco Inc.**
www.berroco.com

**Brown Sheep Co. Inc.**
www.brownsheep.com

**Caron International**
www.caron.com

**Coats & Clark**
(Red Heart, Moda Dea, TLC)
www.coatsandclark.com
www.modadea.com

**JCA Inc. (Reynolds)**
www.jcacrafts.com

**Lion Brand Yarn Co.**
www.lionbrand.com

**Louet North America**
www.louet.com

**N.Y. Yarns/Tahki-Stacy Charles Inc.**
www.nyyarns.com

**Plymouth Yarn Co. Inc.**
500 Lafayette St.
www.plymouthyarn.com

**South West Trading Co.**
www.soysilk.com

**Spinrite Yarns (Bernat)**
www.bernat.com

**Universal Yarn Inc.**
www.universalyarn.com